OTHER STATES OF MIND

First published 2014 by
THE RAG AND BONE MAN PRESS
160 Rodger Road, Panton Hill, VIC 3759
Visit our website at www.ragandboneman.org

National Library of Australia
Cataloguing-in-Publication entry

Title: Other states of mind : stories of mental health / edited by Natasha Bernard.

ISBN: 9780992584597 (hardback)

Subjects: Mentally ill--Biography.
                Mental illness
                Mental health.

Other Authors/Contributors:Bernard, Natasha, 1984–, editor.

Dewey Number: 616.8900922

Publisher: Keira de Hoog

Editor: Hannah Mae Cartmel

Designer: Leigh Rubin

Typeset in Candara, 9.5pt.

OTHER
STATES OF
MIND

STORIES OF MENTAL HEALTH
compiled by Natasha Bernard

PUBLISHER'S NOTE

The Rag & Bone Man Press Inc. is interested in publishing books for change and opening up discussion on global and local topics. Our aim is to collect and publish the stories of people who make up different communities, presenting them without agenda or politics—just in the spirit of sharing. In purchasing this book, you contribute to the continuation of these significant projects that help us all understand and accept each other.

www.ragandboneman.org

THE RAG & BONE MAN PRESS

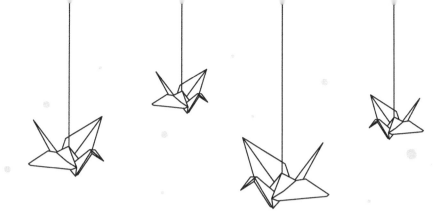

ABOUT THE EDITOR

Natasha Bernard is a registered nurse and has worked as an educational play therapist at the Royal Children's Hospital in Melbourne, providing individualised learning plans for children, to promote effective coping skills, education about their illness and medical procedures through developmental and medical play.

She has also trained as a teacher, a research nurse and is the granddaughter of Anna, who suffered from paranoid schizophrenia for over forty years. Through her vocation, research and personal experience, she is passionate about promoting mental health education for those who have, or care for someone with, a mental illness.

MENTAL HEALTH

The psychological state of someone who is functioning at a satisfactory level of emotional and behavioural adjustment.

Oxford English Dictionary

THIS IS
MENTAL
HEALTH

The state of being at an optimum
level of psychological health

The state of waking up

The state of drinking water

The state of eating

The state of leaving the house

The state of the day where
it's all a little bit fuzzy and
the sound of a laugh could
inspire you to kill

The state of hyperactivity

The state of repeated activity

The state of inattention

The state of inertia

The sound of white noise:

'How are you going today?'

How are

Howaaaaa

Hjy ghe srwgr ewrtre

The state of stasis

The state of silence.

Here is selection of things to do when facing mental health issues:
exerciseeatwelldon'tdrinktoomuchortakedrugsmakesureyou
seeyourfriendsandensureyouarebusyormeditatingthengoforawalk
andtakeupyoga

Here is what you actually can do when confronted with a mental
health problem:

fight

function

do your best.

Mental Health

The state of living a life so relentless

hilarious

Bitter but exceptional

Hard and inspiring

Yes bad, but very very good

The state of emerging

Of crashing

Returning

The state of accepting

And working

And yearning

Of hoping and being

And waiting and seeing

Of striving

And dreaming

Or simply completing

The everyday state of living.

CONTENTS

CONTENTS

PREFACE

NATASHA BERNARD

My story is not special, my story is not unique, my story is not more important than the next person's. However, the inspiration for this book about mental health comes from personal experience. I am the granddaughter of someone with schizophrenia, and my oma has inspired me to compile this book of stories about mental health. I hope that this book will decrease the stigma of mental illness and increase the awareness of the issues that families, friends, carers and the people living with such illnesses face on a daily basis.

The aim of this book was to find the stories behind the statistics. Statistics show that mental illness does not discriminate—from the wealthiest to the poorest, from the city to the country, there is a massive spectrum of stories to be shared, and this book displays the courage, kindness and idiosyncrasies of people's experiences of mental illness within our country.

I have only ever known one oma. The oma who would idle away the day sitting outside smoking Longbeach cigarettes until her fingers were yellow and her daily cigarette limit was up. The oma who would call all the doctors 'bastards', especially the ones who came to give her injections. The oma who would move from boarding home to boarding home. The oma who would just walk, for hours on end, in the heat of summer or the cool of winter, walking away from her terrors. The oma whose eyes would show such fear when 'the lady' was 'coming to shoot' her. The oma who climbed a barbed wire fence and broke her hip trying to escape from the lady who was trying to shoot her. In my haunted grandmother's mind she was always in fear of this lady carrying a gun. My sister and I learned from a young age how to ward off Oma's anxiety and reassure her that no lady would shoot her. At times it was difficult for me to comprehend that, as a child, I was the one comforting an older member of our family. How could an adult be so fearful of something not real? I couldn't understand this illness—which my mother told me was called schizophrenia—and how it was so cruel and terrifying for my oma.

The illness took away the person I would never know. My sister and I were always intrigued about what oma was like before she got sick, we would pester Mum to tell us stories about Oma singing, dancing, fishing for eels and cooking up a storm for Sunday dinner. At times my sister and I would get glimpses of this old Oma, when she would laugh and her eyes would light up. It was as though the true Oma was hidden behind the illness, or the medication. Oma was always a part of our lives and we would always include her in conversation, even if we didn't always get a reply. Oma would visit us at home, come to dancing concerts, graduations, horseriding events and birthdays. Mum would always make special trips to include Oma, make her part of our family.

As an adult now, looking back, I cannot comprehend what it would have been like for my mother to lose her mother to schizophrenia as she did when she was a teenager. My mother's capacity to bind our family with grace, love and steely determination ensured that our family's experiences felt as normal as the next family's.

My mother would always ensure Oma's schizophrenic behaviours were dealt with, with minimal interruption to our family life. Mum managed Oma's illness and still found the time to devote herself to her two daughters and my father. Mum never complained or got angry with Oma, she always looked positively at the curve-balls thrown by Oma's schizophrenia. I am so proud of the dignified way my mother continued to love and care for Oma, through thick and thin. Sometimes we like to look back and have a laugh over stories about Oma, such as the time she flew to Amsterdam for a week to escape the 'lady' or the way she would turn her nose up if Mum brought a different brand of cigarettes.

I hope this book will give people an insight into the lives of all people who have a mental illness, and into the families and carers who are by their sides. When I was researching this book I found common threads through all the stories. I hear about the shortage of adequate services and support, lack of true understanding from some families and friends and the high cost of support services. I hope this book inspires others and the community at large to share their stories with each other. Share the funny, sad, trying and true stories that surround mental health. These stories will bind us together and allow our community to grow stronger and more accepting.

ANNA'S STORY

MARION BERNARD

We have to stick together and make the best of what we can,
as no one knows where this journey will take us.

My mum—Oma to the grandchildren and Anna to everyone else—suffered from schizophrenia. Paranoid schizophrenia to be precise—there, I said it! That name, that illness, would not so long ago put terrible stigma on a person and their family members. So no one would use it and anyone who knew about it stayed away from that person as if they had a frightful, infectious disease. Worse still, if extended family members overheard conversations like 'Did you know she is funny in the head?' That was enough for a once-sociable family to become distant and unsociable. Could you blame anyone? Well, what the hell is schizophrenia or paranoid schizophrenia anyway?

How and why does a person suddenly develop irrational thoughts, become obsessed with paranoid ideas and feelings of deep sadness?

To go back over the past is like unpeeling many layers that have been closed off as the years have moved on.

Anna was born in Amsterdam on 26 June 1922, a second child. Her mum and dad lived in a very poor suburb of Amsterdam, where her father worked in low-paid labouring jobs and her good Catholic mother gave birth to children in a yearly procession—18 in all. Not all of the babies lived, but at any one time there were many more bodies in their cramped house than it could possibly hold. Children slept head to toe, several to one bed, and those who missed out slept on mats on the floor. Anna and her older brother had the responsibility of helping the family care for the children, clean, cook and wash. Money was always very tight, with little coming in to feed the family. When times got desperate, Anna and her brother had the job of rolling up the carpet in the lounge and taking it to the pawn shop for money to buy some much-needed food. When times were a bit more lenient they would go and buy back the same carpet. She said 'it was like a revolving door where things moved back and forth but always managed to stay the same'.

When Anna spoke about her family, she sadly revealed a very strict and strap-wielding father, who followed the instructions of the local parish, even if it meant her poor mother could not cope with the daily grind of looking after so many children. Unlike her father, Anna had feelings of warmth, love and sympathy for her mother.

Anna had gone to school but left early. Her family needed money and it was her duty to help provide for the family.

As time passed Anna obtained a job in a cigar factory, wrapping and packing. Anna was angry that she had to hand over her hard-earned money, and her mother negotiated that she be able to keep a few cents so that she could buy her own clothing.

Anna was 18 in 1940 when war broke out. For the next five years, she and her eldest brother struggled to help feed the family. They often took long journeys on their bikes, riding without rubber tyres over cobbled roads to the countryside, working for farmers and saving some of their food rations to take back to their brothers and sisters. During this period they lived with fear, anxiety, cold and hunger.

It is here that my mother's life story is a bit sketchy, but I do know that her mother passed away with the youngest child only 18 months old, one of her much-favoured sisters, Susan, contracted TB and was placed in a sanatorium, and Anna married a young sailor in an effort to start a new life. She tried to keep her siblings together the best she could and was the key carer for her sister with TB.

Unfortunately for Anna, her married life was not the one she had often dreamt about. It turned out to be a replica of her past, with a strap-welding husband. Anna had two daughters in this marriage—her first daughter carried the name of her beloved sister Susan, who had passed away a few years prior, and her second daughter unfortunately died from a bout of croup. Following this death, Anna was broken-hearted. She always carried a locket of her daughter's hair in a special wooden box.

Anna still continued to clean for extra money during her turbulent marriage and it was when she was hired to clean for a gentleman, Cornelius Riethof, who was recuperating from a throat operation, that her life changed. Cornelius was born into a Protestant family, where religion took a backseat and family took first place. Violence was not part of this family's vocabulary—only kindness, patience, calm and a fostering of listening and talking. A way of life Anna had not known before.

Cornelius had his own history and a marriage that had ended after the war. Cornelius, or Cor as he was known, was slowly recovering with the help of Anna who was hired to assist with the housework and cooking.

Anna was drawn to Cor because for once in her life there was a place without violence. There is no doubt that the talking and listening between them during this time unveiled their troubles and an attraction grew that eventually lead Anna to leave her husband and move in with Cor. They married, my brother Bob was born and I followed a few years later—I was the first girl born in my father's family of all boys—and my mother still helped look after Cor's three sons from his previous marriage.

But things were still very tough. Billboards advertising Australia, showing sunshine and palm trees, started to appear everywhere. My parents decided that it would be a great start to a new life for themselves and the plan was put into action. It was a very difficult decision, as they knew that they could not take their children from previous marriages with them. The final decision was made to go, and that in itself is a story of heartbreak, abandonment and sadness for the ones left behind.

In January 1960, Cor, Anna, Bob and I arrived in Melbourne, Australia after a six-week journey by ship. We went in the same direction as all other new immigrants and travelled to the Bonegilla hostel then got residence at Holmesglen Immigration Camp.

Eventually we moved into a rental house in an outer suburb of Melbourne, before moving into our own home. This was a very happy period in Mum's life and even up until this point there had been no obvious signs of mental illness or feelings of sadness. Dad made furniture and Mum bought new mattresses, a television and a record player with lots of records—music at last. Life was wonderful!

Suddenly, as Anna was approaching middle age, events seemed to unfold from day to night with a blink of an eye. She had been seeing a doctor for a general feeling of unwellness, and one night that doctor arrived with two ambulance officers who, upon entering our house, were faced with one very angry mother. Before I had any idea of what was happening, they'd put a straight jacket on Mum, and she was quickly taken out into the ambulance and driven away.

A feeling of bewilderment and fear engulfed our household, with no idea of what had happened. Poor Dad had to try to keep the family going, one day to the next. To help me overcome my fear for Mum, Dad made a pact that we would visit her every night after school, as well as weekends. That was enough to stop the tears for a while and allow me to get back into a daily routine.

The drive each night was a three-hour return trip, and as tired as he must have been, Dad kept his word to take us every day. The first visit was the worst. The sign read 'Larundel Psychiatric Hospital'. My instincts told me that this had something to do with being 'funny in the head' and my fear and despair grew as we were ushered through door after door, each one being locked behind us as we moved to the next. Then, after the last door, there was Mum, I raced to embrace and kiss her, she was as happy to see me as I was her. Our embrace ended and I moved aside to let my dad greet her, but as Dad went to embrace her, she pushed him away and started to accuse him for getting her locked in this place. She went on and on, and yelled at Dad, blaming him for everything. I just could not understand what was happening—Mum had never been like this to Dad. At the end of our visit, Mum grabbed my hand and said to me that she had to get out of here and that this was no place for her. I had to help her get out. It was a burden I felt way beyond my control.

I felt bewilderment and loss, my brother and dad were mostly speechless and distant. To ease our pain on our journey home, I remember saying that once mum comes out of hospital, which would be very soon, she will be much better; I believed that most people who go to hospital come out better than when they went in.

The year was 1972 and the word schizophrenia was not often used. Mental health was not a topic for discussion and people with mental illness were generally disowned and locked away. There were no doctor, hospital or family meetings, no information for treatment, therapy, support, medication or cure. It was the start to our journey from knowing nothing to uncovering a person who was split in two.

Our visits to mum continued and things did improve. As treatment took place so did her transition to the next level of accommodation. Rooms were sparse, one steel bed and one steel bedside table. There was a greyness and boredom that seemed to resinate throughout the hospital. However, as Mum progressed from one section to another, she gained more freedom, with access to outside gardens, communal rooms and additional activities.

Mum was released from her first stay in Larundel, but her happy, smiling and singing persona never returned. For some reason, I felt that I might have been to blame for her illness and I tried endlessly to make Mum happy—cleaning the house, making her new curtains, buying her flowers and presents—but nothing seemed to work. Mum blamed Dad for getting her admitted to Larundel, and her stories started to increase, with lots of negative things always directed at Dad. For a period of time my brother and I did not know if what she was saying was true or not, but as she repeated these lines so much, over and over every day, it was easy to be swayed into believing her, even though none of it made any sense. My brother Bob was so distraught at home that he had to go and live with some friends for a while. I started to seek sanctuary in school and in friends who were unaware of my saga at home.

My dad eventually confirmed what I already knew deep down, that all the negative things that Mum had spread about him were just not true, but were in fact due to her mental illness.

'When will Mum get better and how do I cope?' I asked him. While still holding me, he said 'Remember this: while your heart might be crying, let your face always be smiling. We have to stick together and make the best of what we can, as no one knows where this journey will take us'. He was a man who possessed absolute positivity; he became my rock. In light of his sufferings—many years at war, a previous marriage breakdown, a move to another country, and only memories of his other children, he was now suffering another blow, the mental state of his wife Anna.

While I was waiting for Mum to get better, the years rolled from one to another, and she only seemed to get worse. Her accusations of Dad trying to poison her increased to include neighbours and other friends.

In learning to cope with Mum and my own life, I went to see a local doctor, who was kind enough to explain schizophrenia in simple terms—the medication that she needed to take and the possibility that she may require hospitalisation from time to time. Any other questions regarding the return of the 'old Mum' just could not be or would not be answered.

Mum went from being paranoid some days to hysterical, agitated and depressed. When she did take her medication, she seemed to improve, but then she'd stop, only to lapse into periods of despair.

These periods could see her back in Larundel for a short period, and then back home again. Once when she returned home from one of her inpatient admissions, she started to blame all the doctors who were now chasing her and trying to poison her.

Anna certainly had a split mind—when she was good, you felt hopeful, and then when she was bad, you wondered for how long this time.

My brother and I eventually met partners and married in the same year. We both moved out of the family home and poor Mum went to pieces. One day when Dad came home from work, the house was empty. Anna had organised a truck to pick up the furniture and store it somewhere. We had no idea where she went. Eventually I got a phone call, it was Mum and she was safe. I found out that she had left because she thought people were after her and if I didn't tell anyone she would tell only me where she was. She was living with the nuns in Fitzroy.

Even though my mum had changed, I always felt a connection between us—I loved her, she was my mum.

After Dad died, Mum's illness took her to live in many places around Melbourne, interstate and even one expedition back to her homeland that lasted only one week. Luckily for me, even if I did not hear from her for a while, she would always make contact with me again. Actually I was the only person she would eventually contact, no matter where she was. My brother and I organised endless trailers and moved her from one unit to another all across the suburbs, hoping and praying that this was going to be the last time. But the moving went on and on and on.

It was the voices she heard, the lady that was going to shoot her, that caused the moves. Sometimes she would call the police, telling them there was someone outside who was going to shoot her, only to find that, after too many calls, she was taken back to Larundel by the same police she had called.

After each release there was yet another place. One time, it was coming up Christmas and she had been placed into boarding house accommodation in Elsternwick. My husband and I went to pick her up to stay at our place over Christmas, but when we went in, I found her sitting with her head in her hands, in tears, surrounded by drunks, with urine and faeces smeared all over the floors. We could not leave her there, so we put her belongings into a bag and left. She stayed with us over the Christmas period and then I had to find a new place for her. She was penniless, but I managed to find a place in the eastern suburbs where I could keep a closer eye on her.

Eventually, when Anna was in her mid-sixties, the nursing staff organised a person from the Peter James Centre in Burwood to look after her. This was the beginning of our journey to assistance and support. Thank God for Peter James!

When Mum needed to be admitted, she would go to Peter James, and when she moved out, the social workers would find her a new place to live. They would also organise visits, meetings, medication, rehabilitation and any support she needed.

A weight had been lifted off my shoulders!

By this time I had two gorgeous daughters. It didn't matter where Mum was during these years, I always managed to have her around for birthday and Christmas celebrations. My girls grew up knowing their Oma, who was sometimes different, but part of our family.

It had taken me many years to come to terms with the fact that my mum suffered from schizophrenia, it took me even longer to ever tell anyone else.

Over the years I had learnt a lot more about her illness. Just like someone who has a parent with kidney disease or heart disease, there are others who have a parent with a mental illness. I wanted my family to accept Anna for who she was—warts and all—I wanted her to be treated like a member of the family, not to be locked away and forgotten.

There came a time that Peter James had no alternative but to place her into their long-term facility. Facilities for people with schizophrenia are nearly non-existent and the majority of people in this facility had Alzheimer's disease. As she was still mobile and enjoyed conversing with people, it was not the ideal place for her. To make her life a little more enjoyable, I would pick her up and have her over the weekend when she wanted to stay. For the times she could not come home, the girls and I would take her out to the shopping centre for her favourite dish, fish and chips.

One day I got a call from a doctor at Peter James who said he thought that Anna should not be there and suggested that I find some other accommodation for her. After seven years in Peter James, the thought of moving her yet again panicked me. I had no idea where to start, but I knew that the doctor was right, this was not Anna's last place of residency.

As it happens, I was driving along Mt Dandenong Road, worrying about whether I'd find suitable accommodation for mum, then low-and-behold a shiny beam came down upon a sign that read 'DutchCare'. As I passed the lovely looking aged-care facility, I wondered if they might consider taking Mum. I turned my car around, parked, gathered my thoughts—practising my sob story, I could even burst out crying if I needed to—and went in. After I explained a bit, the friendly receptionist called their admitting officer who came surprisingly quickly to see me. Sitting down, I divulged my desperation about finding new accommodation for my mum, who was lovely, mobile, could look after herself, was Dutch and … suffered from schizophrenia. And, with a tear in my eye, I mentioned the doctor at Peter James who had said she needed to be out within a few weeks. I was beside myself with worry, grief and fear that they wouldn't take Mum, but before I knew what was happening an arm came around me, with the warmth and friendliness I needed, responding to my plea with a 'yes we can take her'. I felt I had just won Lotto!

I raced to Peter James to tell Mum where she was going—her own room and a new residence with the people from her home country. We were both very excited, but we would have to wait until an assessment was complete and a room became vacant. Luck was on our side—after two weeks I got a call at work to inform me that a room had been vacated and Anna could move in on Friday!

I let Mum know that I would come over Friday morning to help her pack and take her to her new room at DutchCare. When I arrived there was no need to pack, as Mum had the nurses up all night packing her things. After seven years of wonderful care and friendship, it took only a few minutes for farewells and Mum was in the car ready to go.

Mum liked her new room and over time we filled it with her own furniture, pictures, photos and nic nacs. DutchCare had a designated place for Anna to smoke her cigarettes, and this made her even happier.

Over the next seven or so years, we continued to visit Anna, taking her out shopping so she could have her fish and chips. After she had a fall and could no longer leave the premises we still visited each weekend.

As the girls got older, they would still visit her at DutchCare. They were au fait with Oma's split personality but they never knew which one they would find until Oma's initial greeting. In one version Oma would always ask 'How are you going? How is school and when are you getting married?' The girls would answer her questions, and giggle at the last. On these visits the girls knew Oma was well. In the second version they would find a non-responsive Oma with no greeting at all, so the girls would initiate the greeting and ask 'How are you today Oma?' A grumpy, negative response would be returned—one that the girls would often laugh at was 'Bastards, they are all bastards'. This summed up her condition so nicely that we would all burst out laughing, and before long even Oma would have a big smile on her face. She knew in that moment of clarity that she was still part of our family and loved.

The ups and downs of her schizophrenia never subsided—regardless of medications, counselling or electric shock treatment—and never lessened with age. The cycles just kept on going round with no beginning and no end. I finally came to accept my mum the way she was and I loved her just the same.

The voices and paranoia finally evaporated and disappeared the day Anna passed away in April 2012. She was two months short of 90. She now rests in peace—rest, my dear, rest!

It is very difficult to tell anyone about schizophrenia and what it is like living with a person who suffers from it. To this day, I acknowledge that I still don't fully understand it myself. I can only wonder—abusive childhood, war and starvation, abusive marriage, or just life?! How can it be that one minute she is communicating to you about everyday things, then the next, yelling out 'Can you hear her? She is going to shoot me'?

Contra to my previous belief, experience has shown me that schizophrenia is not really like any other disease at all—the brain is the master organ of the body, it can refuse to take medications, have explosive uncontrollable moods, be unpredictable, cause physical outbursts, have no insight or understanding and can make absolutely no sense at all.

People who suffer from schizophrenia need to be treated in a specialist hospital by staff with special knowledge, skill and understanding.

Even though Larundel hospital was initially a frightful place to visit, over a number of years it did serve and tend to my mother's needs. To have had my mother admitted to a general hospital during an 'episode' would have been a frightening ordeal for the other patients who might have found themselves sharing the same room, not to mention the medical staff who sometimes required security guards to be called upon.

The lack of support and services out in the community once patients were released showed a huge deficit. Ex-patients would flounder, feeling stressed and uncertain, being non-compliant with medications and sometimes homeless until their next admission. The anxiety and distress that these events often bring upon the whole family is immense and confusing.

Aged care finally offered excellent services, support and assistance to us, but should sufferers have to wait until the age of 65 to get adequate help? We don't leave a person with kidney disease until the age of 65 before they can access dialysis or a transplant.

Society is becoming more educated and more aware of mental illness, but the lack of support for sufferers under 65 and their families still remains.

I hope that by sharing Anna's story, I can help others become aware that anyone—from any level of society, at any age—can develop a mental illness. And a mental illness, like all other illnesses, disorders and disabilities, is simply an ingredient of humanity.

My enduring thanks to all the staff of the Peter James Centre, DutchCare and to my family.

KINDNESS

KINDNESS

CAMPFIRE

IV drugs in, IV fluids on, old chest drains out, new chest drains in; no fat, high fat, low fat diet; stiches in, stiches out; beep beep ... disconnection of the electrocardiogram monitor, blood tests, medications, physiotherapy, occupational therapy, art therapy, play therapy, speech therapy ... any more therapies and I'm going to scream.

What does this person want of me NOW?! Always someone coming in with flowers or toys trying to 'cheer me up' but I don't care I just look away. I look at my mum and wail—she will comfort me and tell them to go away.

Stale sterile hospital air blocks my nostrils. When will I be able to smell my hair the morning after a campfire? Or smell my fingers after rubbing eucalyptus leaves? Smell the forests and deserts of my home. Instead the smell of disinfectant is seeping into my pores. What is happening to me anyway?

My eyes are blinded by the beeping machines and torches used by nurses in the night. The only way I know to get staff to leave me alone is if I avoid eye contact with them, then I can go back to staring out the window. I want to sleep under the silence of pitch-black sky just Mum and I, looking for the Southern Cross.

Months of pain, surgeries and being held in this room ... what is the point? I can't run through the sand, scream and giggle, swim in the rivers, pick flowers or make a campfire. That is all I want to do ... make a campfire.

I want to feel like I am back at home, back with my family.

A nurse starts to pay more attention to me. She sees that I don't want to play with toys she brings me. I need something more than medicine or food. What I need is out the window, past her head. The nurse with the caring smile turns to look where I am looking. She says 'I know what you need.'

My dreams become a reality, twisting and turning the bureaucracy of the hospital to make me well again.

Out at the campfire in the middle of the park, we sit with the hospital rising up in the background. In the heart of the big city, it's not much like home, but the wind is in my hair and in my mind I can see cockatoos diving and singing. The smell of eucalyptus is somewhere far away and I can see my family, my roots. This is finally giving me reason to smile, and I look at the nurse to make sure she knows my mind is freed. I will look up from now on and look people in the eye, to talk and smile, to forget the pain and therapies and frustrations of the last few months. My spirits are lifted. I know my body will get better because my mind is at peace again.

DID THEY CATCH THE MEN WHO MURDERED GOUGH WHITLAM?

NATASHA RUBINSTEIN

I was reminded of a lost puppy as I watched Paul wander the aisles aimlessly—tail between his legs, easily frightened and instinctively distrusting of those around him.

We were greeted in the dining room by a cluster of confused faces that had turned their attention away from their soup to gape at us. They sensed the intrusion. There was no sign of Paul.

We walked up a creaky narrow staircase towards the balcony. He was sitting outside with a friend, smoking a cigarette. 'Ester!' he exclaimed as he saw my mother approach. He had a slow rhythm to his voice. I'd always thought my uncle sounded a bit like Darth Vader.

I could tell he recognised me but couldn't remember my name. His facial expression was full of childlike eagerness.

There was a large hole in his faded blue jumper and his thinly woven pants stop jaggedly just above his ankles. His hair frayed in random spurts like weeds on top of his head.

Mum placed a box of my father's possessions on the ground next to him.

'We brought you Simon's clothes in case you needed them,' she said.

His friend introduced himself as Jimmy. He talked at us for a length of time about nothing in particular, clearly enjoying the experience of having a new audience.

'My parents never visit me, isn't that sad?' Jimmy told us. A mixture of guilt and discomfort coursed through me. 'But my brother comes. He gives me pocket money.'

Paul offered each of us a cigarette and we politely accepted. The wind blew against us with great intensity, thwarting my attempts to light my smoke. I took it as a sign that there were forces working against my choice. The door squeaked back and forth while we attempted to make idle chitchat. Paul's eyes widened in distress as I retold a story about my wallet being stolen.

Mum butted out her cigarette and cocked her head to the side. 'We were thinking of taking you to the supermarket. Would you like that Paul?'

We'd been told that he liked shopping trips.

'Yes, very much!' He smiled enthusiastically.

Mum offered to drive the five-minute walking distance. Paul paused his slow shuffling into the house to consider his options. 'It might rain. The sky looks treacherous.' He looked upwards and raised his eyebrows discerningly.

At the bottom of the stairs was a 'smoking kills' poster with an accompanying diagram of facts. I smirked at its redundancy. Smoking seemed to be one of the few things keeping most of them going.

The drive was mercifully short. As we got out of the car mum urged me to hold Paul's hand. 'He's probably afraid of traffic,' she whispered to me. I grabbed onto his jumper lightly, unsure of how he'd respond to the physical contact. He gasped suddenly, stopping dead while a nearby Toyota almost reversed into him. I pushed him forward gently, coaxing him toward our destination.

His relief upon entering familiar territory was noticeable. I wondered how often he ventured outside his residence, and how far he actually went. We went into the nearby Coles and headed straight for the confectionary aisle. Paul followed cautiously in anticipation of his treats.

'Mint Slices?'

'Yes.'

'Tim Tams?'

'Yes.'

'Cadbury Favourites?'

'Yes please!'

We'd also been told he liked to share the box of Favourites with his fellow residents.

Paul mumbled to himself at random intervals as he pottered through the supermarket, his bony ankles barely covered by navy blue socks. It was at this point that the tirade of odd questions began. 'Were the Jews black, white or brown?'

Mum answered directly, 'Well, there are Ashkenazi Jews of Eastern European heritage, and Sphardi Jews from Africa ...'

'Did they catch the men who murdered Gough Whitlam?'

'He's still alive as far as I know, Paul.'

With a poised rationality and patience she has reserved for a situation like this, Mum continued answering his questions. Soon though they became so nonsensical it was impossible for her to answer, so she just nodded and hummed in agreement.

I was reminded of a lost puppy as I watched Paul wander the aisles aimlessly—tail between his legs, easily frightened and instinctively distrusting of those around him.

There was an off-putting aspect to the width of his eyes, the height of his eyebrows, the depth of his gaping mouth. Supermarket-goers and attendants subtly gawked at him, and rapidly focused on ruffling through their trolleys when I made eye contact. I could see that to them he was a wandering strange man—someone to fear, not the fearful.

We got to the check-out. Mum shouted him a packet of Benson & Hedges when we discovered the brand he requested didn't exist.

We drove back to his residence, and it seemed to take longer than before. Paul had regressed into silence, not even asking questions anymore. We parked the car and Paul opened the door; he smiled at Mum and thanked us.

'It can get lonely by yourself,' he said, and patted me on the head before disappearing through the gate.

I COULD SMELL FLOWERS

SKYE HARTUNG

I was in Albury-Wodonga and they had tulips and small yellow flowers that were just lovely.

I couldn't smell flowers all through my 20s. Simply, I was always off my face. I was healing, but it was slow and painful.

I started seeing a psychologist in my early 20s. Whatever state I was in before, I got significantly worse from this experience. Psychology pushed me to relive a lot of my childhood. I don't know if my memories were repressed, but bringing them back up didn't seem to help. It came to the point where I was afraid to leave the house my anxiety got so bad.

I was taking anti-depressants off-and-on-again but, like a lot of people with mental illness, I'd been self-medicating with alcohol for a long time.

They've proven in psychology that when horrific things happen, whether a natural disaster, a war or a personal trauma, going to a counsellor and speaking about it doesn't always help in the short-term. In the long run it does and is necessary for your future happiness, but there's a lot of trust involved. Trust that it won't always hurt so much. Trust that reliving those events will enable you to move past them.

It's a full time job, understanding your own illness.

At roughly age seven, my innocence was taken through sexual abuse by a cousin. I also had physical and mental abuse from my father.

When I was eleven I went to a party in Sydney and got really drunk. That was the first time I picked up alcohol for myself. That was also the night Mum found out Dad had been unfaithful to her so she was drunk herself.

My whole family drank. It wasn't uncommon to go to events with a few bottles of something under your arm. I brought myself up because Mum wasn't coping, but neither was I, and so I developed a daily need for alcohol.

Reliving these events opened my eyes to the vicious cycle my life was in. My father wasn't good to me during my upbringing, so I entered into relationships with people who weren't good to me. When I was 18, this reached a peak with a boyfriend who physically abused me. Finally seeing the pattern was good—you can't break free of something you're unaware of. And, when it mattered, I had the support I needed.

'Love, I really think you need to get help.'

My GP has known me since I was a child and was very thorough. This helped in a huge way—doctors at the GP level need to be educated to know when/where to refer people for mental health treatment.

Even still, my depression went undiagnosed for a long time. I had an unhappy childhood, so whether it was situational or biological, it would be hard to tell at what stage it manifested. Whether the alcohol came in too soon, the stress was too much or the depression was always there, I just don't know.

Recently, I've been classified as bipolar as well. I'm still coming to grips with the label; it manifested itself very differently to how people might think. My mania, as it was described to me by my psychiatrist, is like being highly strung. I'm unusually tense and irritable. In the midst of my mania my mind races with:

**OHMYGOSHIFONEMORELITTLETHINGHAPPENSOUTOFLINE
I'MGOINGTOCRACKEXPLODEANDLOSEIT!**

Being labelled as bipolar seems severe. But it's easier to treat now that I'm correctly diagnosed and since starting on the medication for bipolar I'm feeling much better and my depression levels are much lower.

I asked my husband, 'How do you think I've been?' and there was silence.

Depression is like nothing else. Everyone has sad moments, but when you're depressed it's like a heavy weight covering you. Regardless of anything, I couldn't get out of it. Being a mother stops me from mentally dying; it's a reason for living because I've got to get up whether I like it or not. Still, my worst bout of depression came after my second child was born. I fell into a major clinical depression; I could barely walk, read, write or talk. I remember trying to type on the computer, but when I looked down at the screen it was just a jumble of letters:

**Kajdw; 21019jdfm room kfdhg oeot 20jkf
ppa lfpqmi9v l]-2fh j**

It was like I'd lost my motor skills. Everything was in slow motion. But the worst part—I couldn't be the mother I knew I was capable of being.

*The towel is rolled out onto the grass and I am lowered onto it.
My family is around me, giggling, playing, kicking a football.
'Mummy, Mummy!' my little girl drops the ball next to me.
I don't flinch; I say nothing.
I sit on the towel while life whirls around me.*

My husband stayed through my alcoholism. Our marriage was very rough during that period. But his mother also suffers from depression and so he's sensitive to it. If it wasn't for their support and the support of my own mother, I would have been hospitalised.

My husband always held my arm. He helped me move when I was too weak to walk.

Again I asked my husband, 'How do you think I've been?' and he grinned.

I'll always remember smelling the garden outside the rehabilitation centre. I was in Albury-Wodonga and they had tulips and small yellow flowers that were just lovely. My creative senses all came back. I felt liberated. No matter what happens in your life, whenever you can, enjoy these simple things.

My mother-in-law organised for me to go to rehabilitation. I will always thank her for that. It was after a lot of damage had already been done in our family. I broke down crying because I knew she was right. I didn't want to leave my daughter, she was so young, but I had to go anyway.

After the decision was made we organised a flight and a place for me in the centre straight away.

I was away for three months, but the healing was instant. It's one of the most significant periods of my life, cleaning myself up, finding out who I was. When I bent down to smell the flowers at the rehabilitation centre, I was happy. That place was like a church, awash with light. I cried for two days straight, the scent of yellow petals hanging in the air.

I felt liberated.

I have a mental illness, so sometimes I might slip up, but I'll never dwell on the shame again. There's so much shame involved in addiction, it creates a self-perpetuating cycle. Now, I get back up. Back then, that meant fixing my marriage. Now, I can turn my life experience into something that might help others.

I have one subject left to finish my Bachelor of Psychology. I started it a few years ago and, because I've got two young children, I study part-time. I've also enrolled for a Master of Mental Health for next year. My main focus of study is in mental health and alcohol, and mental health and crime.

I want people to know that there's always hope. No matter how bad your childhood or upbringing has been, whatever you're feeling will fade.

I was lying back in bed with my husband one night. I said, 'I'll just listen to a bit more of this', and I smiled as he groaned out loud—another online lecture (and a boring one). But I kept on studying through every phase of my illness—even when I couldn't type, walk or speak. I went out to work at the age of 14 and didn't get to finish my junior certificate. It's my time now!

'How do you think I've been?' I say. 'How good or bad have I been?'

I don't know how many times I've asked my husband that question and how many different responses he's given. I will always ask it, because when you're sick it's the people around you who see how you're doing.

'You know what,' he says to me now, 'you've been happier. You've been better.'
I can't see that, but I trust him and it's important for me to know.

If I could change one thing in my childhood, it would be communication. I wish someone had told me more about what was happening. Mum could've said, 'Skye, your dad and I are having problems, but I love you. I know it's hard for you to understand, but I'm not going anywhere and you're safe.'

I think a good childhood is about the explaining of things. Proper communication would've made me a wiser child and perhaps less immature in choices I made later on. It definitely would have impacted my future.

My children don't know much about my illness—they're still young—but with a psychologist for a mum and a teacher for a dad we hope they'll be OK!

When I met my husband he was a musician, the drummer at the back with his sticks going crazy. I remember the first time I saw him I knew there was something special about him. Corny, but true. We were married in our late twenties, had our daughter at thirty and now we're thirty-eight and life is good.

Life is really good.

by Allie Brosh hyperboleandahalf.blogspot.com.au

∏O EXIT

Felicity's story, interviewed and written by
M A D E L E I N E   L E W I N

---

*Felicity shared an anecdote with me that signified the first moment she
saw her mother in the vulnerable light of her mental illness. To Felicity this
moment acts as a signpost in her life to the moment she was forced to
grow up and lose her childhood naivety.*

My mum and I are off to see *Letters to Juliet* at the movies. We head for the nearest
cinema, hidden somewhere inside a huge suburban shopping centre. We can't quite
remember where though. Was it behind the K-Mart? Or perhaps it was near the food
court? We park at the other end of the building, check the centre map and figure out
that the only way to it make there is through the IKEA. Not exactly a straightforward
route, but a decent chance to stock up on a tealight candle or two.

We don't rush. Mum seems more than happy to browse and there's still 15 minutes
before the film begins. Plenty of time.

Somewhere between the orange napkins and the five dollar towels, though, I realise
that ten minutes have passed.

'Almost time for the film to start mum, we better make a move.'

Mum and I look for a way out, but each doorway leads us into another room, and we
find ourselves going in circles, with no exit in sight. As we hit another dead end, I notice
Mum beginning to panic. She grabs my hand, forcefully. Her breathing becomes heavy,
short, as if someone sealed off the ventilation and cut off the air supply. She groans
and trembles and I start to wonder if she's going to burst.

Glancing back at my mum, she is suddenly a child. Vulnerable. Defenceless. I start
to go numb, but instinct takes over. I realise that I have to act quickly. Grabbing her
by the arm, we charge through the store, winding past endless displays, through

crowds of oblivious bargain-hunters. Rushing and searching, I feel like I'll never find anyone who can help us.

Finally, an IKEA employee comes into my line of vision.

'Excuse me!' I manage to blurt out, 'Where is the exit to this store?'

The man turns around and looks, first at me, then at my mum's panicked face. She squeezes my hand in an iron grasp.

'Ah … um … just this way', he replies hurriedly, sensing the urgency in my voice.

My mum continues to hold on to me, terrified, as we dash past couches, through bedrooms and around kitchens. Eventually, we arrive at the exit.

As we follow the IKEA man out of the store, the final light whimpers of my mum's anxiety fill my mind. A strange sensation, a feeling of a loss of innocence, begins to creep over me. Coming back to my senses, I realise what I had just witnessed. I had witnessed alone, properly and for the first time, my mum's mental illness, the symptoms of her depression and anxiety, at its rawest.

RU

OK?

I HAVE NO FRIENDS

I don't have any real friends, people who aren't my family, who ring up to ask me out. I don't blame the world for this, as I can't make eye contact with people and, after all, 'eyes are the window to the soul'. I can't gain enough courage to make conversation in a group situation so I always look down at my feet. People feel awkward around me and so they don't bother to make more than a passing conversation. I think they think I am simple, uneducated and that I'm too mentally unsound to make a friendship with. I speak too softly to be heard in a crowd or across a table when people do ask me a question, so they just give up. Anyway, I give some strange answers sometimes when I can't understand what people are asking or know what answer they want me to give.

When I was young I had some school friends. They were the country type of kids that would let me join in a soccer yard game or let me hang on the edge of the group following them around. I would get invited to the occasional kid's party, but mainly only because the whole grade got invited.

I'm good-looking I think—shiny hair, nice eyes, white teeth, a little on the short and stocky side but I know girls will give me a quick glance sometimes. But it seems they soon make the connection that I'm not like the other boys. I don't respond. I don't make eye contact. I don't speak up. They soon move on. I don't even think about having a girlfriend now.

My siblings have lots of friends. They are nice to me but they are not really my friends. I can never share a beer with them (because of my medication) and I can't stay up late (because I need to have a pattern of sleep).

I went to a self-help group once to try to make friends, but it was religious based and I believe in science not religion. My parents joined me up to all types of sporting groups—football, basketball, tennis, cricket—but none of the people I met have ever rung for me to come over to their house to socialise. I can't get on the phone to ring people because I don't know what to say. I get anxious.

I'm not sure what will happen when my parents die. I will not have many people who care about me then. I will have my siblings, their partners and future children. Maybe their children will grow up to like me too.

I have tried classes to improve my conversation and eye contact. But I can't seem to put the lessons into real life situations. I think my mum wishes there could be a group of really friendly people who would make a genuine connection with me and would ring my phone to organise to go out with me each week to the pictures, bowling, footy or something (to give my parents a rest).

I guess I will be single all my life.

I am told I have a mental illness.

I don't believe this.

But I take my medication because it makes my parents happy. If my parents and siblings are happy then I'm happy.

I don't really have any friends.

BONNIE AND SERENA

N A T A S H A   B E R N A R D

People don't want to know about the bad stuff ... unless it is really extreme. Mental illness is a difficult subject. It's a difficult subject to explain and it's a difficult subject to understand. Mental illness is invisible, it's not an illness where you can look at a person and see it ... so it's not an easy thing to explain.

I first met Bonnie in a busy restaurant on the outskirts of Melbourne. I was excited to hear this passionate lady's story, but nervous and anxious at the same time. As I walked away from our chat I felt more determined to collect as many stories for this book as possible. To get the stories out there to allow other people in the community—who have or know someone with a mental illness—the opportunity to learn from others and seek reassurance that they are not alone. Bonnie's positivity and strength has enabled her to become a successful career woman, a loving mother to Chantel and a grandmother to William, Alex and Christopher.

THIS IS BONNIE'S STORY ...

My mum, Serena, has schizophrenia and now she has Alzheimer's, further compromising her quality of life. I always knew there was something different about my mother—I would go over to friends' houses in primary school and I could see that their families were different. I used to think I would really love a family like that, with a mum and a dad, and a brother or sister. My household always had a stressful, charged energy—my mother's illness often plunged her into fits of rage as she battled the demons in her head, the voices that rendered her paranoid about the world around her. She would leave cryptic messages for me to decipher—I could never make sense of them, she would sit on the end of my bed in the middle of the night and I would wake to find her just sitting there staring at me, ready to tell me about the demonic angels and ideas floating around in her head. I would get so mad at her. I started locking my bedroom door, seeking peace from her ranting. One night, in a fit of rage, she took a hammer to the door to try to get into my room. It was very frightening.

I was very fortunate that my grandmother lived with us—she provided solace in my childhood, she loved me dearly and offered security and companionship. She'd comfort me when I was the focus of my mother's rages. She would say, 'Don't worry, she is mad'. Reflecting on this now, I have come to realise that she knew there was something wrong with her daughter.

I believe my extended family always knew there was something wrong with my mother. My uncles cut her off entirely, and as a result I also lost them as part of my family. They used to live down the road, but they distanced themselves from 'the mad sister', 'the mad Serena'. They were embarrassed and angry.

When I left home at 16, I was very angry with my mother. I had a personal battle to get myself housed and educated. I married very young, trying to build a family for myself, the sort I was seeking to have as a child. My mother was very disinterested in my life, she was highly psychotic most of the time and very difficult to be around. When I had my daughter she showed no interest in her newly-born granddaughter and did not meet her until she was 3 or 4 months old. This was fairly typical of her demeanor and attitude towards me. As a consequence, I didn't see her much throughout my 20s. But when she got diagnosed I found the ability to forgive.

My mother didn't get formally diagnosed with schizophrenia until she was 63. I am not sure why it came so late.

Her diagnosis came after she had an altercation with the neighbours—the police were called and they realised she was unwell. They took her straight to Larundel, the psychiatric hospital. She was involuntarily committed and was there for nine weeks.

I would visit her every day in Larundel. It was a horrible place, the smell was stomach-churning, but it did have a place in our system, to help stabilise people and get them long-term psychiatric care. I can remember going there and having the first meeting with the psychiatrist, and they actually put a name to it. When they said the word 'schizophrenia' it was a big shock. It sort of made sense but the initial reaction was just shock.

The psychiatrist said to me, 'So when did your mother first get sick?' and I said, 'Oh I don't know, she has always been like that!'—I will never forget the look on the psychiatrist's face! It was then that I realised my childhood had actually been very abnormal.

The diagnosis sparked a journey for me. I went looking for information about schizophrenia. There was so little information about the disease back in the early 1990s and what was available was very focused on the sufferer—there was a little bit for parents who have a child with a mental illness' but no support or information at all for children whose parent is unwell. The dynamics are very, very different when it is a parent. The children are so often silent victims and their lives are anything but normal when they are being raised by someone with a serious mental illness.

I feel sad that the illness has robbed my mother of so much—being a mother, and a grandmother—it has taken things from her that you and I take for granted. There's nothing you can do. Mum is on high levels of anti-psychotic drugs, but the drugs make her zombie-like—she has no motivation, she can't do anything, she doesn't want to do anything. So there is a limit to the quality to her life.

Sometimes you get a good day and you cherish them because they are few and far between. My grandchildren love her, they have no preconceived ideas of who she was before being diagnosed. We all visit her in the nursing home, they will take her by the hand and walk around the garden talking and giggling. These are the moments to be remembered and cherished.

Living with a mother with a mental illness forced me to grow up a lot earlier than I should have. I have learnt resilience, forgiveness and understanding. I believe it has made me a better parent, grateful for the privilege. I am dedicated to my beautiful daughter and grandchildren and lucky to be very engaged in their lives.

I have spent the last 20 years trying to find a way to have a relationship with my mother, despite her illness. I feel I am more sympathetic now to what she has been through in life—I want to find some sort of core that is her and not the illness.

I have come to believe that she would have been a wonderful mother had she not been sick.

I love her.

SECONDARY SLUMBER

E L L A   M I T T A S
from an interview with Gabriella Mirabito

I used to stress over the fact that so many of my friends and relatives had mental illness and that I would be next. Then I was diagnosed with depression and anxiety, panic disorders and insomnia. I started to see the school's counsellor after a rather large argument I had in year 7 and it developed from there. I confided my feelings to a close friend and she pushed me down the hallway and into the counsellor's office and made sure I stayed there until I booked an appointment. My counsellor was really fantastic, she was always there for a chat and I'd feel amazing after a session with her—it was great to have someone who listened to me and tried to sort out what was going on in my life. I continued to see the counsellor from that day, once a week during the school year until I was in year 12.

Heading into year 12 I guess you could say I hit a wall. I lost passion for everything I enjoyed. Instead all I did was sleep ... endless hours of sleep.

When you're sick, sometimes the hardest part is accepting that you're sick. Once you've got your mental illness you don't actually notice that you're sick until someone says to you, 'Stop, take a look at yourself, you're actually doing something that's bad for you'. At first I didn't want to accept that I had anything wrong with me. There's a history of problems in my family—schizophrenia, psychosis, dementia, depression, autism and bipolar. Most of the people who brought me up have had a mental illness, which worried me, because those people aren't the same as when I was younger. They've basically all disappeared in a way. I spent so much time hoping that I wouldn't get sick and when I did it was hard to acknowledge.

At first I tried to keep my mental illness a secret from my family. I didn't want to put extra pressure on everyone with everything else we had going on. I had to tell them eventually, and my family having so much mental illness ended up being a blessing. Because we've had so much experience with this kind of thing we know where to go and what to do, which can be hard to figure out if you've never dealt with it before. While I was being diagnosed my school attendance wasn't that great and neither were my grades. I was sure that my school thought I wouldn't amount to anything, basically. All I kept hearing was, 'You're never going to be able to do anything,' and all this other stupid stuff. They decided I wasn't coping with year 12, and they just pulled me out. But what I really needed was for someone to sit down with me and ask me how I was going, help me with catching up and explain things to me.

I wanted to be the first person in my family to go to university—it had been my main goal since I was little. So when they told me that I could no longer do year 12, I thought, 'There goes my only dream'. But then I went to an open day where I met someone who told me a few back entrances to get in. They and my family also provided me with enough encouragement to believe that I could study.

Now I have four post-secondary qualifications to my name and I'm in the second year of a teaching degree. When I think back to some of the people at school who thought I wouldn't amount to much I think, 'Hey, I've completed so much more than you thought I would'.

Report

by a psych nurse at a hospital

We had a 17-year-old boy last week, whose story upset most of the staff. He had a history of anorexia and bulimia, self-harming and multiple suicide attempts secondary to depression. He has had four ICU admissions this year due to overdoses. He was a good-looking young man with horrific scarring covering his arms, chest and legs. His self-harming was extreme, as the scars were thick and jagged (should have been sutured but obviously weren't). This admission, he had filled the bath, taken an OD of anti-depressants and cut his wrists. Mother found him semi-conscious and called an ambulance. His whole family must have been through hell, along with him. I wonder if it crossed her mind to stop the suffering and go for a walk around the block, finally giving her son what he wants. I guess it's hard to know unless you are in that position. We had him ventilated in ICU for 24 hours. Overnight we lessened his sedation as we planned to pull out his breathing tube in the morning. As he woke up he just lay there crying because he was still alive. It was very difficult deciding how to relate to him. Because he is my son's age and not unlike him in appearance, I just wanted to take him home and mother him. But I doubt that or any medication will help this boy. Most likely he will get what he wants before Xmas.

ANIMALS

I have two dogs and playing with them is the best thing in the world, for happiness. Without them, you've got no one to talk to and they don't care what you say. They don't expect anything back.

It doesn't matter that they don't talk because it's just someone there to listen to you when you're sad or depressed; it's just company. People don't always understand that sometimes it's just being there that matters.

Dogs are great because they can listen and they're good at knowing if someone's ill or has a depressed mood. When you're down they want to come up to you and lick you and things like that, to say 'Look, I'm here to look after you and to protect you'.

People are more ... they hide within themselves in a shell when they're sad. And other people don't always know about it. But animals catch on to moods quickly. They don't worry about the shell too much.

My friendship with my dogs is a loving and warming friendship. Every time we go for walks I feel really happy because I'm giving them the time to be free. It feels really good to look after them. When we play together it's like playing with a child a bit. No expectations. They like their environment as much as children do. It's simple to make them happy. It's also easier to interact with people when you're walking a dog. You can focus on the pets and talk about them, rather than about yourself.

They give dogs to some prisoners to get them to be motivated again when spending their time in prison. They should do that more in hospitals. They do it in lots of nursing homes. It keeps all the people cheerful.

Being around animals gives you a chance to rest.

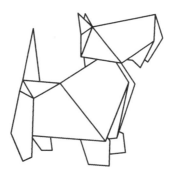

DEPRESSION CROSSING

BILL WOOTTON

must have been my fault

I the unknowing cause

of this this gridlockdown

this deep and until just now

unshiftable mood mire

listen now

words pass

unloadedly

for a while

where's the we I thought we had

either end of the bridge we are

are we crossing together ever

or only meeting in the middle

from time to time

and withdrawing

to our sides

MUM AND ME

EMMA B

---

*She always puts others first and I know that the love
she has for my sister and me is unparalleled.*

MY MOTHER HAD ALWAYS BEEN DIFFERENT TO OTHER MOTHERS.

On reflection I think I'd always known this, but didn't quite understand why. It wasn't until she had a breakdown when I was 23 that I found out she had apparently suffered from this condition her whole life. She was diagnosed as having bipolar, with a slight trace of schizophrenia. I was very fortunate, in that my mother's bipolar was never ever aggressive. She was, and always has been, extremely loving and supportive. Her bipolar takes the form of extreme highs and lows, but with no aggression towards anyone.

IT'S UPSETTING HOW QUICK TO JUDGE SOME PEOPLE CAN BE.

Throughout my primary and high school years we were part of a Seventh Day Adventist community. Although the adults tried to be kind, because they didn't understand Mum or know how to manage her she became too much to handle, and as a result she was often misjudged and misunderstood. Despite all she gave, it just wasn't good enough. She'd always have a smile on her face, but I'm sure she felt it at times. As you can imagine, the attitude of the adults was reflected in their children, so as a consequence I also felt judged.

WHEN MY MOTHER HAD HER BREAKDOWN, I WAS OVER AT HER PLACE EVERY DAY.

Mostly I came around with prepared meals and to ensure the washing and cleaning were done. My mother (and, as a result, my younger sister) didn't like that I was taking on the adult role so I started to back off after a few months. It was difficult, but there was nothing more I could do at that time. They didn't really want my help anymore and personally I was exhausted and needed a little space as well. By that point Mum was stable enough to start doing basic things in her day—showering, eating, washing, sleeping and taking her medication (when she felt like it).

LUCKILY MY FAMILY AND FRIENDS WEREN'T JUDGEMENTAL AT ALL.

When Mum had her breakdown I was very fortunate. My family and friends have always been loving, accepting and tolerant of my mother and I couldn't ask for anything more. If you know someone in a similar situation as a carer and you're at a loose end about what to do, I can tell you that food always helps. Knowing that my mother and sister had good meals at home helped to take some of the load off.

THERE ARE MANY TIMES WHEN THE ROLES REVERSE AND YOU FIND YOURSELF PLAYING THE PARENT.

I guess you grow up a little faster in some areas than you may like. When Mum had her breakdown it was exhausting both mentally and physically. Sometimes it's like you're hitting your head against a brick wall. You can feel very helpless. It's also frustrating as there is privacy between the patient and health professionals, so they may not tell you everything, and the various specialists don't always communicate with each other. Another challenge is that there is such a major lack of resources and programs for integrating people like my mother into the community. I believe there needs to be greater community awareness to break down the stigma surrounding mental illness and to facilitate understanding, acceptance (by this I don't mean accepting negative or abusive behaviour) and management strategies.

I AM THE FIRST TO TELL HER OFF AND THE FIRST TO STAND UP FOR HER.

I still have my days when it's hard for me to accept how she is. Growing up, I remember wishing she was more like the other mothers. But I look back and know my mother gave (and continues to give) my sister and I the most important thing—love. She always puts others first and I know that the love she has for my sister and me is unparalleled.

IT'S BEEN A ROLLER COASTER RIDE, BUT THINGS ARE IMPROVING.

I am so grateful for my family, friends and all the health professionals who helped my mother get to this stage. It has taken years, but thankfully she hasn't had another breakdown as bad as the one I experienced with her. She has moved on to incorporate non-traditional therapies (like massage and meditation) has found a doctor who she trusts and what seems to be a very supportive friendship group. Mum now has a stable routine and is looking after herself. She is happy, and that's all I could ever ask for.

COMMUNITY

COMMUNITY

THE HEART OF THE COUNTRY

N E R I D A   A N D   B R I A N   E G A N

It's 5 am and we are out of bed and having a cuppa before we start at 5.30 am on our property, shovelling feed for our starving cattle—an exhausting task as both my husband and I are in our 60s. The shovelling and feeding goes on until about 10.30 am and by then we are totally done in. But we believe that if we look after our cattle, they will look after us. And, really, the drought is not about us but about the cattle, as they are the ones who feel the real pain of hunger. That's why we go out every day and face that, and feed them.

Drought is like a cancer—the longer it goes on the more insidious and debilitating it becomes. It attacks every part of the body, you lack the energy to do more than the basics, every part of you aches and it dominates your life. Even though we do not have cancer, that's how we feel.

Farmers take a huge sense of pride in their work and because of this, as well as their isolation often in small towns or on large properties, most don't like to ask for help and simply suffer in silence.

'We contact families discreetly who may need help and are too proud to ask,' says Brian Egan, who started Aussie Helpers in 2002. 'We work around three words—*care, share, respect.*'

Brian grew up in country NSW and Queensland and is a veteran of the Vietnam War. He lost his own farm near Dalby in Queensland in the 90s from a combination of drought and personal depression. Brian was hospitalised in 1999 at Greenslopes Hospital in Brisbane, suffering from severe depression and post-traumatic stress disorder. The mental illness took three years out of Brian's life.

After recovering from this ordeal, Brian and his wife Nerida felt that no organisation was doing anything significant to help families suffering the full effects of the worst drought in living history. So they set up Aussie Helpers—an organisation of volunteers that set out to help farmers out of poverty and lift the spirits of those severely affected by drought in the outback.

'Nerida and I heard many stories of hardship during the drought,' says Brian. 'One sticks in my mind about a 21-year-old girl who lived on a property badly affected by drought with her brother and parents and grandparents. They ran beef cattle and merino sheep but their hayshed was empty and their paddocks were mostly dirt and the family were resorting to cutting tree branches to save their stock. They were really struggling and her father mentioned selling up or putting all the stock down, as they could not feed them. But she did not want to lose the place that had been her home for her entire life.'

'Aussie Helpers assisted this girl and her family, with loads of hay for their cattle and assisted the family in general with visits and counselling, as well as supplying them with goods for everyday use. This family and this wonderful young lady have survived the drought conditions and all the emotional turmoil that drought creates. Bush people are tough and tenacious, and the family really only needed a bit of help to get over a few bumps in life. Aussie Helpers were the only organisation that answered their calls for help, so we were proud of the successful outcome.'

Brian estimates that more than twenty lives have been saved from suicide and hundreds have been assisted with face-to-face counselling.

When Brian was very ill with severe depression a clinical psychologist gave Brian the following advice, which Brian has followed for the past twelve years—'Go out and find someone worse off than you are and help them'. Brian says that Aussie Helpers is his medicine and doing positive work takes all negativity out of his mind.

For more information or to volunteer or donate, go to www.aussiehelpers.org.au

Photos by Andrea Hayes—Outback Photography

THE HAIRBALL

K A T H R I N E   C L A R K E

interview with a mental health nurse

In general I've realised that for Indigenous people it is not just the individual that experiences this suffering—the whole community also becomes affected.

When you're a mental health nurse, especially in remote Australia, you get pretty used to the bizarre.

A co-worker once told me of an Aboriginal man who had a mental illness and suffered over fifteen pseudo-seizures. Strangely, once he was admitted to the clinic the doctors monitored him for a while but couldn't come up with a diagnosis. They thought there was nothing seriously affecting the man and causing the seizures, so they discharged him, prescribing medication, which he took, and he left with an assigned nurse to monitor him at home.

The man's family were not happy, as you can imagine. So they decided to handle it themselves traditionally.

His family invited an Elder from a neighbouring tribe, who is known for traditional healing. He performed a spiritual ceremony, which culminated in the Elder reaching over and pulling an actual ball of hair out from the man's head.

It seems far-fetched, I know. To be honest I don't really know if this is what really happened. My first thought was that it's possibly a kind of placebo, just from believing. Or maybe it really is something that we of the Western culture would consider magic.

One thing is for sure—you cannot deny the strong spiritual connection Indigenous people feel towards each other, the land and their culture.

As far as I know, the clinic and practitioners leave the man alone now because he is coping fine. He continued to take his meds for a short while after the hairball event but he hasn't suffered from another episode since the Elder treated him.

This is one of many reasons I believe there is a difference in mental health between non-Indigenous and Indigenous people. Many of us living in a Westernised society generally view mental health as something that is properly managed if an individual is diagnosed with a disorder and quickly treated with a drug.

For many Indigenous Australians, mental health includes social and emotional wellbeing, which is external and internal for them and their loved ones. The element of spiritual healing is what makes Indigenous mental health differ from Western mental health and is another natural alternative for Indigenous Australians who are not used to the prescribed medication.

Indigenous people, from what I have seen and heard, look at mental health from a united and holistic perspective.

Like anywhere, when it comes to an individual suffering from a mental disorder, there is always some stigma—some families disown people who are suffering, while other people are accepted and cared for.

But in general I've realised that for Indigenous people it is not just the individual that experiences this suffering—the whole community also becomes affected. Many issues that trigger mental illness for Indigenous people are caused by the influences of the past, which carry through to present generations. It impacts heavily on the individual and their community.

The advice I'd give to other mental health nurses like me, who work with Indigenous Australians, is to be consistent with their support. I had to understand and consider different situations and backgrounds when working with Indigenous people, as it is vital to first be aware of the customs. There are many Indigenous communities, and they all have different ways of handling issues such as health. It would be ignorant to think that all Indigenous people are the same.

From what I've seen, Indigenous people in remote Australia believe there is a spiritual reason that someone is suffering with a mental illness, such as a curse or punishment that has been placed upon them because they have done wrong within the community. There is a belief that those who are suffering can only be cured through traditional practices, and once all evil has dispersed from the body the individual and community are safe again from any danger.

Traditions and spiritual practises are common and still continue to thrive within communities. Traditional healing is used as a way of fighting away bad energy, and hair isn't the only thing they'll discover. Stones or even black smoke, which I heard smells putrid, is expelled from their bodies after the ceremony is completed.

One method used around here is water. There are many swimming holes and waterfalls in remote Australia, and for the locals, water is used as a cleansing of the spirit and self. Each place has a significant spiritual connection to the people.

I haven't been invited along yet as I am only their nurse and we need to stay professional. But if I were one day in the community and not working I would love to spend time learning more from them. One Indigenous community may share similar principles to another but even then they are practised in a separate manner to a neighbouring mob. I cannot speak for the nurses who work with Indigenous people in other remote or urban communities, as all communities differ and you'll learn something new and rewarding from each.

There is something about working here that feels sacred and untouched. It is a welcome feeling that humbles me. For the Indigenous communities in remote Australia, I have discovered there is a thirst to understand and support one another. They carry each other through the struggle of pain and suffering, which is something you don't often find within the Western world.

3 MATES 7 SEAS

BENJAMIN ROBINSON

There is a crack, a crack in everything. That's how the light gets in.
⁓ LEONARD COHEN

I never thought a bunch of teenage strangers would inspire me to do anything. If you told me they would be the driving force behind a dream trip—surfing the 7 seas with 3 mates—I would've thought you were joking and laughed it off. But that is exactly what happened.

After going to a suicide prevention workshop at the University of Wollongong, my mates and I were shocked to hear that so many young people were taking their own lives. What hit pretty close to home was that many of the young people who were dying were much like ourselves—15–24 years old, male and from regional Australia. As we chatted with each other about our own upbringing, similar stories began to emerge. Even though the problem seemed pretty big, we still wanted to help change it. Somehow.

Fortunately we live on a pretty big island in Australia, surrounded by 3 seas—the Southern, the Pacific and the Indian. So, on our way to surfing the first 3 of the 7 seas on our trip, we also visited some 60 schools across regional Australia. We were not psychologists or psychiatrists, so we based our school talks around building resiliency techniques and used our 2-year 7-sea odyssey as a metaphor for their final (and often most challenging) 2 years of high school. Triple J picked us up and the ABC followed us everywhere—(surprisingly) the talks were a hit.

It was not until we were over half way through our trip—the honeymoon period was well and truly over and we were stranded alongside our crashed car in the Sahara desert—that we realised the momentum our project had gathered.

After spending nearly 2 years on the road together, our friendship and the project's meaning was barely recognisable to us. The 3 of us were done, we just wanted to quit and go home.

But our website was still receiving encouraging remarks from the students we visited and, while the trip was turning in on itself, we found ourselves going to the website for encouragement. The support of the students got us through to finish the trip and surf all 7 seas around the globe. It was pretty humbling to receive a comment on our webpage from a girl whose mum had recently died. It shocked us to hear her thank us for sharing our story with her and how it helped her to have a laugh at a low time in her life.

Nearly 2 years after we left our hometown, we returned having surfed all 7 seas. We crashed 3 cars along the way, narrowly survived the Sahara, got scared out of the water by sharks, got robbed and nearly had our boat capsized in the stormy Indonesian waters. But my greatest challenge was still to come.

After returning home, I didn't have many goals and I fell into a deep depression. I could not find a good job, I had very little money and I began to withdraw from my partner and social settings. I stopped surfing. The next 12 months got really tough. Luckily I was dating a psychologist at the time and she recommended some people I should go and have a chat to. I saw several psychologists until I found one I connected with, and saw a psychiatrist who prescribed me some medication. But sadly, on more than one occasion, I planned how I was going to take my own life. The very thing I spent 2 years raising awareness and funds for was the same thing I found myself suffering from.

Slowly, though, the fog lifted. I began surfing again, I armed myself with good food and I ran 3 times a week. Even though my mind was telling me to stay indoors, I pushed myself to go and catch up with friends. I began to laugh again, instead of cry. Around the same time I attended a cognitive behavioural therapy course at the Black Dog Institute in Randwick, NSW. It did wonders. This is why 50% of all DVD sale profits of our documentary—3 mates 7 seas—are being donated to Black Dog.

We only made this documentary years after our trip, as I grew stronger. We put a teaser of our doco online, to see who might be interested in helping us produce the 80 hours of raw footage we had. I sent a copy of the teaser to some 50 production companies I had never met before. Even though our teaser got over 10,000 visits on YouTube, we only got one reply. Her name was Loosie Craig. After meeting her, we knew Loosie and her partner Mark Alston were the right team. They just got us—like we had met before or something.

It sure is surprising how big your goals can get when you are in good mental health. Conversely, when I was suffering from a mood disorder my goals of getting out of bed and having a shower sometimes seemed out of reach. This is when my life has been the most challenging.

I see mental health as not unlike physical health—if you don't exercise, you eat bad foods and don't prioritise your health, you will get sick. Mental health is no different. Resiliency-building is something I try to incorporate in my everyday life and, when I get the opportunity, this is what I convey when I talk to groups.

Follow the journey and purchase the DVD at:
www.3mates7seas.com

ISOLATION

RAELENE HALL

Depression is a medical disease—it is not a figment of your imagination, or you going insane or just being lazy, useless or hopeless. The symptoms are as varied as the people who suffer it.

But what is depression for me?

I am a woman in my 50s, living on an isolated cattle station in the East Gascoyne region of WA. My nearest neighbours are over 100 km away and the nearest town (a small outback town with limited facilities) is 210 km away.

I didn't put a name to it until I was in my 40s. Even then I had trouble accepting it—not that I was depressed, that was a given—but that it was a medical illness and nothing to be ashamed of or embarrassed to talk about.

I had an alcoholic mother and only in recent years have I realised she was also depressed, probably for most of her life. What came first—the alcoholism or the depression? One inevitably feeds the other. My feeling is the depression came first. The loss of her third child and first-born son could well have been the catalyst. She just had to absorb her grief and get on with life. My father blocked out the grief rather than sharing it, so two people who were hurting were, tragically, unable to comfort each other.

DEPRESSION SCARES THE CRAP OUT OF ME.

It is such an insidious disease that can creep up on me unawares, even when taking my medication. One day I'm feeling fine—the next, don't want to get out of bed, have no motivation, life seems pointless. Questions reverberate around and around my head. What use am I? Why am I here? Would anyone really miss me if I weren't? Thoughts that I know are wrong and stupid because, yes, my husband and kids, my family and friends would miss me—I know that for a fact but it doesn't seem relevant at the time.

'What's wrong?'

'I don't know.'

'Are you sick?'

'No/yes/I don't know.'

'Can I help?'

'Yes/no/I don't know.'

Nothing is straight in my head. I, who am usually so articulate with words, cannot express what I am feeling. Why not? Because I don't know what it is myself. The frustration of that, at times, makes me want to punch a hole in the wall to see if it will give me some relief from this constant feeling of 'what is wrong with me, why do I feel this way and why can't I stop feeling this way?'

THERE IS NO SIMPLE ANSWER AS TO WHY SOME PEOPLE SUFFER DEPRESSION AND OTHERS DON'T.

For me one of the biggest catalysts for my depression is my geographical isolation. Usually, I enjoy company, conversation, outings, being involved in and organising events.

In the past I've overcome my isolation to a certain extent by becoming involved in organisations like the CWA (Country Women's Association) and ICPA (Isolated Children's Parents' Association). Though I wasn't able to attend face to face meetings it was contact with like-minded people who shared similar interests and also lived in isolation.

For years I taught my children on School of the Air, and this helped keep my depression at bay. I wasn't always the greatest home tutor (too impatient) but it meant being involved in our school (albeit from a distance), having teachers visit us, attending face-to-face events where I could interact with other isolated mums. It meant travelling long distances, but the benefits, for my children and myself, were worth it.

All of these things helped, but I really struggled when my children left home for boarding school.

Then a huge event impacted on the life of rural and remote people—the ban on Live Export. I became very involved in social media as the debate raged on the topic. I found myself connecting and making friends with women right across Australia. We all had the same thing in common—supporting the Live Export industry that so many people relied on.

From this connection I was invited to join a group of around 50 women right across Australia. Our only mission was to be there for each other and have a forum where we could share our stories and offer comfort and support when and where it was needed.

I still don't have face-to-face contact but I think I have the next best thing. I have a group of friends who are not afraid to say it like it is, to share their stories good and bad, to seek and offer support.

I CAN TELL THEM WHEN I'M DEPRESSED AND THEY WON'T TELL ME TO SNAP OUT OF IT, TO GET OVER IT OR THERE ARE OTHERS WORSE OFF THAN ME.

They will just be there for me until I can climb the next depression mountain.

Best of all, I can do this at any time of the day or night. There may not be someone to comment or respond right away but it's rare to wait very long. Somehow it's easier to type how I'm feeling than try to articulate it verbally.

Every time there is an opportunity for members to meet face-to-face it is grabbed and photos are posted so we all share in the joy of an online friendship morphing into real life catch-ups.

These women have helped me believe in myself, they have taught me that sometimes a swear word is the only one to describe this lousy black dog (and some of the idiots who inhabit the world), they accept me for who I am and I, in turn, accept them for the wonderful caring women they are.

DEPRESSION WILL ALWAYS BE A PART OF MY LIFE.

But with the help of medication, a wonderful loving family, some incredibly beautiful and supportive friends and the most amazing online support group a woman could ever ask for, I will continue to find the peaks among the troughs and slowly but surely hope to spend more time on the top of the mountain instead of in the gloom of the valley below.

A JOB TO DO

by the parent of a child with schizophrenia

To most people an 'illness' means a person with a sickness that needs to be cured. But it is possible to be permanently ill—some people are never going to be cured. This is what it is to have a mental illness.

People who are ill are often not employed, because they are likely to need specialist medical help throughout their employment, which is scary for an employer. An employer thinks, 'What if they display some of their illness at work? What if they become even more severely ill? No, don't employ them, that is the safest.'

It's like they don't stop to think that this person takes medication for their illness, that their moods are actually more controlled than the majority of the workforce. They say, 'So what if the person is monitored by a doctor and has a strong family support network?' They think it is better to employ a person with no medical record and no family support and no doctor because they do not have an illness and will therefore never cause a disruption.

Why are people with conditions like epilepsy or diabetes less scary to employ? Can't people with these conditions cause a disruption if they forget their medication too? What about people who suffer from alcoholism or drug addiction? Or even just young people who binge drink and turn up for work badly hungover or still drunk? Aren't they dangerous in the workplace too? What about someone with a gambling problem who steals from the till, aren't they going to cause more problems for the company?

So why do they discriminate against my daughter who has schizophrenia? She has declared it, she is constantly monitored to prevent it interfering in her and other people's lives. She takes regular medication to ensure she is very stable. She is gentle, loving and reliable. She is keen to work and contribute to society. My daughter loves routine and repetition. That is perfect for big companies with jobs that can be very similar day to day. But no one will employ her because, according to the world, she has an incurable illness, while other people only have conditions or unknown personal lives that are much safer for society.

Medication may make a person's reaction times slower—but this should not be a problem if the job is done carefully. Is someone who moves faster but makes mistakes more suitable for a job?

People who have schizophrenia tend to be quiet, hardworking and not into social gossip on the job. They work well under direction and don't tend to step on anyone's toes by arguing that they could do the task in a different way. They are capable of working in a supportive environment where they are given clear directions and tasks.

People who have schizophrenia want to have a job to do.

BIPOLAR BEARS

MICK SEYMOUR

Howdy-do my long lost friends
You're the ones that live in my head
Can't believe you're back again
Last time we ended up in a psych ward bed

SONG LYRICS TO 'SO REAL' BY THE BIPOLAR BEARS

Hi! I'm Michael, drummer for the Bipolar Bears, one of Australia's rock'n'roll institutions. We've been playing our own brand of music and talking about mental health to audiences for over 20 years.

Despite the challenges and problems thrown up by the band's mental health issues, I couldn't dream of being in a better group.

It is hard to do anything at optimum levels when you have a health condition, but I have been in many mainstream bands that don't have the great camaraderie and caring nature of the Bears. Maybe our empathy toward each other has a longer-lasting resonance than just sympathy from others. I have found that sympathy has a short shelf life ('just snap out of it'), but empathy has an indefinite innate mutual understanding.

Too many of us just shut down and hide away and, while that can still be an issue for us, at times we also feel compelled to play our music for our own therapeutic needs as much as for other people. It's a great fact that rock music lends itself well to shouting out and purging painful emotions.

Our guitar player, Dan, wrote the lyrics to my favourite Bears song, 'So Real', based on his own mental health experience. Our bass player and vocalist, Adam, says, 'I find if I don't play music at least every couple of days I start to lock things in and I start to get anxious. Playing music is like an outlet and we like to spread that word to anyone else who is suffering with mental health issues. I know now just how much it takes to get up and lay bare (bear?) ;-) our emotions. I wondered when I first joined whether I would feel a bit self-conscious about being such an open advocate for mental health (in essence, exposing my condition to the public instead of just those closest to me), and yet I am not at all hesitant or embarrassed—instead I am proud.'

What better way is there to engage the community than through a band advocating engagement rather than isolation, and through inspiring others to keep up with whatever creative activities they do?

The Bipolar Bears are part of Wild@heART Community Arts, a fantastic organisation creating arts participation opportunities for people who experience disability or mental health issues. Please visit www.wildatheart.org.au for more information.

BLOKES LIKE ME

ALAN GREENHALGH

A tale about how men's sheds save lives.

Sixty-year-old Bill Bailey reckoned he'd reached his use-by date. Who wanted a clapped-out old fart, forced out of the workforce by a succession of debilitating health conditions?

Answer: no one.

Unemployable and unwanted, he'd joined the sad, ever-growing pile of baby boomers languishing on life's scrap heap. But for Bill, the worst part was losing contact with the adult male world, along with his usefulness to society. Despite living in a metropolis, he felt as lonely as a desert island castaway. 'I should change my name to Robinson bloody Crusoe,' he mused.

While Bill's wife Jill enjoyed good health and found fulfilment at her job, Bill wiled away his days at home trying to seek purpose in mundane household chores while battling chronic pain. Although he tried his hardest to remain cheerful, the pain had taken its toll. And he'd been stuck in an endless game of doctor ping pong, being bounced from specialist to specialist without relief. All this had converged to make him a grumpy old bastard.

As time progressed, Bill's sense of isolation and loneliness worsened, and depression started to make its mark. In the middle of the night when the pain was at its worst he'd gaze at the valium bottle and wish he could end it all, but Bill refused to take this path. As an ex-copper he'd witnessed first-hand the devastating effects of suicide too many times to do that to his family.

'What's the point of it all?' he enquired of his own reflection one morning while scraping off his sandpaper-like stubble. Looking back over his life Bill reflected on his hard, miserable childhood. As the youngest of three boys he'd been physically beaten, bullied and mentally abused, not only by his father but his elder siblings who'd taken their lead from a parent who lived by the adage that 'children should be seen and not heard' and certainly not praised, indulged or encouraged to realise their true potential.

In later years Bill would come to understand that his childhood was not unique. Consequently, he didn't expect any sympathy and he understood that, like it or not, what happens in one's formative years often determines the direction one takes for the remainder of life. Kicked out of home as soon as he was of employable age by a father who regarded him as nothing more than a financial burden, he'd fended for himself from the tender age of fifteen, living in various seedy boarding houses in Sydney's western suburbs.

Life in a big city was hard for an introvert with little self-esteem. Bill battled loneliness and difficulties in stoic silence until depression finally led to his first suicide attempt. Swallowing a handful of over-the-counter medications in the hope they'd bring about an end to his miserable existence, he had collapsed alone on the cold boards of his boarding house room. Sinking into the abyss, the fear of dying alone and friendless briefly shocked him back to consciousness. What if one didn't simply disappear into oblivion? What if something worse waited for him in the afterlife? What if he didn't die but inflicted so much brain damage on himself that he became a dribbling idiot?

Jamming his fingers into the back of his throat, Bill gagged and vomited his stomach contents onto the threadbare rug beside his bed. 'Wake up to yourself, you useless bugger!'

In the hopes of starting anew Bill bought himself a one way ticket to Auckland. There he worked a series of odd jobs, and got married at age 18 to a controlling Catholic girl named Mary. Bill and Mary had a couple of kids and moved around a lot, and eventually life took him back to Australia. Knocking around WA with his family dragging behind, Bill tried his hand as a bar manager, as a commission salesman and as a security officer at the famous Argyle Diamond Mine in the remote Kimberly region of WA. Meanwhile, tongues were wagging behind Bill's back about Mary's tendency to drop her knickers for any man except Bill. Predictably, their marriage broke up.

For Bill, the break-up was akin to striking gold. He was free at last to make his own choices and pursue career goals. And he fell in love with a lovely lady named Jill.

Taking up a position as security manager for a major state government institution was the beginning of Bill's decline, both career and health wise. Not one to tolerate egocentric, power hungry politicians with whom he had to deal daily, Bill chucked in the job after a year, figuring he'd be better off working for himself.

Unfortunately his first venture, a high pressure cleaning and truck detailing business subjected him to a variety of toxic substances which ruined his health, bringing on an acute case of chronic fatigue and fibromyalgia that was to continue wracking his body with pain for years to come. Selling the business before it killed him and ruined Jill and him financially; he struggled with various ventures until he finally became too weak and ill to work.

Wiping the remnants of the shaving cream from his now-smooth face, Bill was suddenly struck by inspiration.

I've got to stop this downward spiral of self-pity. There must be thousands of blokes out there like me. They're all thinking they're bloody Robinson Crusoe when in fact they are an untapped resource that society should be putting to good use. What's needed is a shed where blokes can go when they feel like it, socialise, pool their skills and help those who are less fortunate.

Hurrying to his study, Bill logged onto the internet. 'Does such an organisation already exist?' he wondered. Googling 'blokes shed' he soon discovered the Australian Men's

Shed Association, an Australia-wide organisation, which at that time consisted of 30,000 members and approximately 500 sheds.

Great, I'll join one.

Unfortunately for Bill there was no shed close by. Undeterred, he contacted the local council whose community development officer greeted him enthusiastically. 'We've been waiting for someone to start up a shed in our area. However, it has to be community driven. Are you prepared to do the work to set it up?' Peta Sopworth asked.

Bill had a pretty fair idea of what he was letting himself in for but he also knew it was a golden opportunity to shake off his malaise and put his various skills to good use. 'I reckon I can do it,' he told her.

'Well, you need to know there's no council land or buildings available and no money set aside for the project. It has to be entirely community driven. But we'll support you all the way.'

Yeah, and how are you gonna do that, then?

After circulating 500 pamphlets mass-produced on his home computer, Bill called a public meeting in the local hall and invited the mayor and local politicians. 120 people turned up and to Bill's surprise so did the mayor and the local federal member.

Bill spoke nervously to a sea of eager faces, boldly announcing the 'shed' was now a reality despite having no money, equipment or place to meet. He recruited six blokes to form a working group whose task it would be to find a home and help with the enormous red tape involved.

Although it would be untrue to say things went easily, within six months Bill's idea had found a home in a disused manual arts section of a local high school and developed into a registered not-for-profit charity. By its first anniversary Bailey's Men's Shed Inc., was firmly entrenched as a resource within the local community.

Nearly four years and numerous community awards later, its 170 members have made thousands of toys for needy kids and performed countless good deeds for less fortunate members of the local community. More importantly it has rescued blokes like Bill from suicide and made significant inroads into tackling crippling depression, social isolation, loneliness, and age-related problems, while simultaneously improving the health and lives of its members and their immediate families. It is now one of over 1000 men's sheds with a combined membership of over 100,000 members nationally, and the movement has been so successful that it has now spread worldwide.

There is no doubt it saved Bill Bailey (and countless others like him).

For more information on men's sheds visit: www.mensshed.org

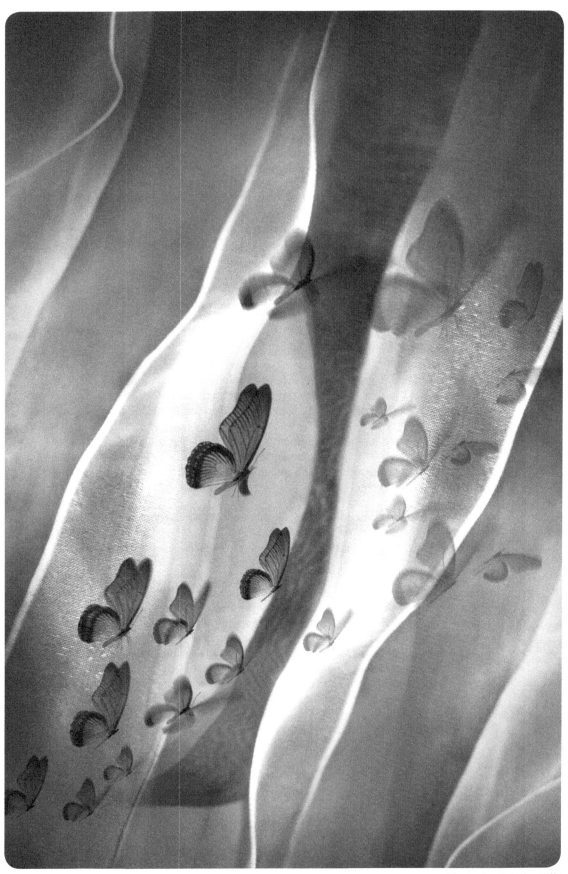

LONG ROAD

SYLVIA KAUER

Ever since I was a teenager I've struggled with depression. At first the doctors had no idea what was wrong with me and I was diagnosed with a range of things like chronic fatigue or seasonal affective disorder, or told I was just being a moody hormonal teenager. Some doctors were kind and considerate, but most were dismissive and obviously didn't know what to do with me. It was pretty tough. I had a few good friends who were nice to me and although they probably didn't understand exactly what was happening, they accepted that I was unwell. One friend sent an enormous bunch of balloons—my friends were going to bring me flowers, but she knew I'd prefer balloons. It was so nice to think that people were concerned and didn't think I was a freak.

Some people were pretty mean though—I was told by a close friend that I was no fun anymore, that I should just try and make an effort. It was an effort just to get out of the house each day.

Over time, things got better. I've been on anti-depressants on and off for years now and while I tend to feel OK when I'm on them, I find the side effects that come with them frustrating after a while. I start to wonder who I really am and want to try and see what I'm like without them. There are times when I'm worse, particularly in winter, when I have a cold or when I'm stressed, and there are times when I think I'm almost normal. But invariably, it happens again. It's a very physical thing for me. I get headaches, general aches and pains and I'm really lethargic. I find myself snapping at the people around me or crying in a corner about something minor, or I start to think how much better off everyone would be without me. It always takes me by surprise and takes me a while to admit that I'm depressed. But then, there I go again, making appointments with my psychologist, getting the latest anti-depressants or sleeping tablets from the doctor, feeling like a failure, getting angry with those around me and with myself for being depressed again.

I guess it was my personal experience with mental illness that attracted me to the field of psychology. I was, initially, thinking I'd like to be a psychologist and help others, but I soon realised that I couldn't handle other people's issues on top of my own. I'd wonder what to tell them when I felt just as hopeless. That's when I got into research. I did my PhD investigating a mobile phone self-monitoring app and how it could be used in the early stages of depression. The app tracked young people's moods, stress, coping strategies, exercise, sleep and diet four times a day for 2–4 weeks.

It was better to sit there and answer that, instead of punching stuff.
(14-year-old male)

The aim was to increase young people's awareness of their moods and factors affecting their mood and ultimately, to reduce depression, anxiety and stress symptoms. After completing 2–4 weeks of the program, they looked at the results with their doctor to see what's going on for them and figure out some strategies for dealing with any issues they were facing.

> *When I was in a bad mood and I had to fill it out, it would make me feel better because I knew that people were going to be looking at it and reading it, reading the mood chart. It just made me feel better.*
> *(15-year-old male)*

> *The summary at the end really put it into perspective what I get stressed about. Times of the day, why I'm stressed.*
> *(17-year-old female)*

We found that the simple act of tracking mood increased young people's awareness.

> *I suppose I thought that it was pretty useful because it was getting me to think about my moods. Usually it would make me stop and think. It made me realise when I was in a bad mood, usually I wouldn't realise that at all, just because it was asking me how I was feeling. It kind of told me that sometimes I had background stress that I didn't really realise was there before.*
> *(17-year-old female)*

It increased recognition of mental health problems, helped to identify problems and the causes of their problems.

> *Sometimes I'd have to stop and think but I suppose it was something at the back of my mind most of the time. It wasn't really hard but it wasn't something that came automatically. I just had to stop and wait a second.*
> *(17-year-old female)*

Some also felt that it helped to think about strategies to cope with their problems.

> *I just would get angry and turn on my music and vent. And then with this it goes 'what will you do now?' Like, I never really think what am I going to do because I'm angry, because I'm really angry. I think it really helped you with different ideas on what you can do and then it'd always ask you if you did that.*
> *(16-year-old female)*

Some of the comments from young people who took part really show the benefits of computer-mediated communication.

> *I liked the benefit of not having to talk, just doing it. I liked that part of it. The 'no talking' thing. It was just like a quiet thing ... I personally find it hard to talk to someone about it ... how I feel and things like that. Whereas you're not really talking, you're just expressing how you feel ... and I liked that better than talking. That's what I liked about it, because I just don't get along with the talking thing. But the writing thing was good.*
> *(16-year-old female)*

I can relate to this young woman, it's difficult and really boring talking about your feelings again and again. We were also pleased to think that the effects of the app might last beyond the 2–4 weeks. One young woman reported:

> *I actually now without it [the self-monitoring app], sit back and think about those kind of things ... about the different things that factor into your mood.*
> *(16-year-old female)*

It has been a long road. I have a good psychologist who gives me useful strategies that help me think in more productive ways. I have a wonderful partner and a great job, which I'm good at, at least most of the time. I know that I will probably get sick again and I watch for signs and symptoms. When I catch myself crying for no particular reason or thinking about terrible things that have not happened yet, I know it's time to start counselling and think about starting the meds again. It still sucks and it's depressing always being worried about getting depressed again but at least now I know to get on top of it early and let the people closest to me know that I'm struggling. I think things are getting better for people with mental illness in general, although there's still a lot of work to do. There are more avenues for people to explore when they are having emotional problems and there are heaps of internet sites and apps that might help too. I'll just keep struggling on, enjoying the times when I am well and trying to overcome my depression when it occurs.

The mobiletype app was developed by Dr Sophie Reid and Dr Sylvia Kauer, at the University of Melbourne in collaboration with the Murdoch Childrens Research Institute, who conducted a randomised controlled trial with 114 young people (14–24 years) in primary care settings.

It is not available anymore although there are several apps that track mood such as mycompass.com.au. Visit http://orcid.org/0000-0001-9797-9822 for Sylvia's academic publications about this app.

OUTLET

At 20 I lost my home and friends in the Black Saturday bushfires.

My fiancé, our 20-month-old daughter and I are lucky enough to tell the tale.

I remember sitting thinking, How are we gonna recover? We aren't insured, where can we go? How can we support a baby with no money, no nothing? Thanks to the bushfire appeal we managed to get our lives back on track financially. But the financial worries I had was the least of them.

I never considered the emotional impact it would have on us—sleepless nights, even the sound of an aeroplane passing by would have me in panic. Eventually after months I could sleep again, but only if my fiancé was there beside me. He was pretty much my hero, and I became very reliant on him.

I started writing blogs and opening up, and eventually I got better. It hit us the worst as the one-year anniversary approached. My fiancé wasn't the same—he was violent, abusive, and a wreck. He shut himself off completely. Everyone noticed it, and it wasn't until recently that he admitted he has a problem.

He saw a doctor and started seeing a psychologist, and slowly the person we knew is returning. I'm also seeing a counsellor. Even though I have an outlet in my blogs, that stranger I can talk to is a great help. I really feel like a stronger person now, not by going through what we did, but by overcoming the emotional obstacles that followed. Even my relationship with my fiancé is the best it has been since the fires. For us, counselling is still an ongoing thing at this point, and I'm positive things will get even better. I'm not scared anymore.

My advice to anyone is to find a healthy outlet. Talk about it, write about it—anything!—and when you're ready, see a counsellor—they can give some great advice. Don't try be the strong one all the time. Break down, cry, throw things, let it out. Then take the steps to recovery. I'm saying this as a 22-year-old, as a friend, as a partner, and as a mother. The best advice I was ever given was 'You can't be good to anyone unless you can be good to yourself'. So look after yourself.

FOREWARNED IS FOREARMED

KATHRINE CLARKE

When I see people with tattoos on their forearms I can't
help but wonder if they are hiding a scar too. Or when
people cover their forearms with scarves, wristbands and
sleeves, are they too covering a past they wish to forget?

When I look at my left forearm, I see a past that cannot be erased.

Growing up, I became quite familiar with bullies and the harm they can do to someone. Because of this, my father wanted me to do self-defence classes. Judo was his answer—'a grappling martial art where the strength of your grip relies solely on the strength of your forearms'. I quickly learnt that the stronger my forearm, the greater the advantage over my opponent.

But that was then. Nowadays I avoid looking at it. Beneath the caramel complexion of my skin, my forearm feels like it's an open wound.

I still remember the first time I sliced my forearm; the cold steel of the tweezers—yes tweezers, I couldn't even find the guts to use a razor. One slice left only a faint red mark. I knew if I was going to do it right I should slice downwards, but I didn't really have any intention of taking my own life. I was numb and determined to feel something. I went to do it again, positioning the tip of the steel on a slant, and this time the blood oozed out. My forearm stung as I let the tears roll down my cheeks, and I smiled. Was I twisted or wicked for smiling like this? My parents and younger brother popped into my head—what would they think? I was ashamed because I enjoyed the feeling; I was obsessed with the way the dark red liquid flowed down my forearm, my eyes fixated on it.

It eased my pain and numbness, but on the other hand it made me angry, knowing instantly what I had done was wrong. Cutting yourself was taboo, mainly because so many in my community have died due to suicide and self-harm. It was around this time our family had lost someone dear to the whole community and it changed a lot of people. Some of us still ain't been the same since. I strongly believed that suicide was the coward's way out, but was conflicted about self-harm. I felt like a hypocrite, preaching against something I did behind closed doors. Nothing justifies it.

Torn within my own mind, the strength I once felt in my forearm was slowly seeping onto the floor of my bedroom and that young girl who loved judo because it made her stronger seemed out of reach.

At 18, I was old enough to get a tattoo, so I chose to cover any sign of this past. But now I just view it as a painted scar. When I see people with tattoos on their forearms I can't help but wonder if they are hiding a scar too. Or when people cover their forearms with scarves, wristbands and sleeves, are they too covering a past they wish to forget?

Mental illness has affected many in the wider Indigenous communities and on a personal level within my own community. Many Elders are still healing from a past they can't erase, but they find happiness in other things such as their arts and crafts. Some individuals struggle with daily issues, and in the end their mind can't handle the pressure. The drugs and alcohol can play a big factor too because they provide a 'quick-fix' in healing some of the pain. Some of the mob fall off the tracks, but in the end many find themselves turning to a family member to get them through their struggles—replacing the negativity with a positive. I think that's what makes us a strong Indigenous community.

If you live with a mental illness it takes time to heal and rehabilitate yourself to what you once were or even half the person you wish to be. As someone who is Indigenous and having gone through a similar situation, I can say that a good ear, from within your family and community, is one key to fighting the fight. If professional help is required, it should be approached with a cultural awareness and sensitivity so that the next steps can begin in supporting people and their communities who are suffering.

I look back now and I know my disorder was depression. I was depressed about my obesity, depressed about my parents' relationship breakdown, and depressed because none of my so-called friends could support me as I supported them. My family issues eventually worked themselves out over the following years. I think the hardest part of it all was admitting I had a mental illness—I didn't even acknowledge the possibility until a counsellor suggested that I take anti-depressants. I had to admit to myself that I needed help. The one thing I can say is, my brother, and my parents, they were the ones who helped me through it all.

Some scars have faded over the past nine years, one has disappeared beneath the black tattooed ink. Like my younger days training in judo, strengthening my forearms in defence, I look at my forearm as a shield prepared to defend me in hard times, a reminder of the lesson I had to learn in order for me to be the wiser, much stronger woman I am today. I also try to assist others in their journey—Indigenous and non-Indigenous alike.

As the saying goes, 'forewarned, forearmed: burnt children dread the fire'.

KEEP TALKING

B E R N A D E T T E   W A L K E R

My husband and I are both fourth-generation graziers.
We live off the land as provided by nature.

Imagine a firm belief—something that you know without question, without thinking. Perhaps you 'just know' that if you take a breath, clean air will flow into your lungs. Or maybe you are sure that the sun will come up tomorrow. Now, if someone presents the right arguments, you can see logically that your belief might be wrong. There is no real guarantee the sun will rise every day. BUT after the discussion, you will probably go back to believing that it does, just as much as I believe the world would be better off without me.

This is a feeling I have held in every fibre of me since I was about 9 years old. And I can function OK, knowing that it's probably not very rational. But as soon as I have a day when everything I do goes wrong, which in my industry is a regular occurrence, that belief raises its head a little higher and it gains a little more weight.

Eventually if I get run down and tired, fighting off that belief can be just too much. It becomes a constant loud screaming in my head that I cannot shut off. This is how my depression feels.

My favourite book is a children's book called *I Just Want to Be Me*, by Tim and Sandra Bowden. I read it to my kids every now and then, but it's really to remind myself of its messages around living with depression. Keep breathing, keep moving towards a goal (even if it's only a goal for the next few minutes) and try to make peace with the monsters living in your head. They stay quieter that way.

My husband and I are both fourth generation graziers. We live off the land as provided by nature—for example, we have some man-made watering points, but once rain stops, it's a finite resource. Please don't harbour romantic notions of stockmen and governesses and cooks etc.—apart from my family, there are no other humans around! I have our three kids to help me run our 100,000 acres but the property barely supports one family, which is why my husband has to have a 'real job' to support us. He works away half the year; for three weeks at a time he is unable to come home.

This lifestyle suits us because we don't like crowds of people or traffic very much. Driving thousands of kilometres to get to the city doesn't scare us. But I have learnt the hard way that I do need social interaction. Coming back to a property after I was married, with a husband away working for weeks at a time, there were times of extreme aloneness. I like being alone, but I have to admit now that it hasn't been good for me in the long run.

There were years where we struggled through medical mismanagement. I was told that everything was in my head, and that I should ignore it and get on with life. This is NOT what you should tell someone suffering from very serious depression. After many years of trying different counsellors—some fantastic, some not so crash-hot—I eventually found that Acceptance and Commitment Therapy (ACT) helps me the most. Living in the country can make finding the right help even harder, and keeping up the energy to search for the right 'fit' for your depression can be difficult. I also find telephone counselling really useful, because the effort of getting kids and myself to town for an appointment can sometimes be too much. Having a really excellent counsellor ring me gives me a huge boost.

I think stigma still exists, but luckily I don't hang out with gossips. I don't care if others see me going to an appointment, or hear me talking about my depression. I have studied psychology myself—if I wasn't in the middle of nowhere I'd probably be a psychologist by now!—and it has helped me to understand there are many ways to treat mental illnesses. I've realised that when a counsellor doesn't work for me, they are not necessarily 'bad'; their theory just may not resonate with me. For example, Behavioural Therapy leaves me cold. It makes me feel as if the way I think is what makes me depressed, and that I'm therefore to blame for my own illness. I have also found that those who have battled depression themselves sometimes make the best helpers.

I owe my survival to my husband, a few fantastic counsellors, and Facebook. I don't belong to any depression groups, but I do belong to a group of isolated women from all over Australia. There are enough similarities to understand each other's struggles and triumphs AND enough differences to provide perspective. I think a 'group for depression' would probably become a 'depressed group', and be too inward-looking for me.

I've learnt that as humans we are social animals—we NEED to interact, we NEED to talk. If you have a mental illness you NEED counselling. Medication cannot be a sole cure.

FUCK UP NIGHT

LET'S CELEBRATE OUR FUCK UPS!

To tackle the rate of suicide among men in Australia, bold new approaches to suicide prevention are required. Suicide remains the leading cause of death for men aged 14 to 44, and 80% of all suicides in Australia are men.

We live in a competitive society where weaknesses, mistakes or 'fuck ups' are covered up, glossed over or ignored, rather than enjoyed for the glorious learning opportunity that they should be.

'Fuck Up Night' is an ongoing, internationally coordinated series of informal events taking place in bars and cafés across the world to celebrate and own the fuck ups we make in life!

THERE ARE TWO RULES:

1. YOU MUST MEET AT LEAST ONE NEW PERSON

2. YOU MUST SHARE AT LEAST ONE FUCK UP YOU'VE MADE

It doesn't matter how big or small the fuck up is. Let's face it—the better we get at sharing the small things, the easier it is to share the big things that get us down.

'Fuck Up Night' is an initiative of Soften the Fck Up and Spur projects.
For more information or to host your own Fuck Up Night, visit www.fuckupnight.com

YOU GOT OUT OF BED

YOU GOT DRESSED

YOU GOT OUT THE FRONT
DOOR

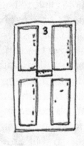

THESE MAY SEEM LIKE SMALL THINGS, BUT WHEN
YOU ARE LOW OR DEPRESSED OR AT WAR WITH
YOUR MIND, THESE SMALL THINGS ARE
ACHIEVEMENTS. SO I'M JUST TELLING YOU,

WELL DONE.

RUBYETC

rubyetc.tumblr.com

A WALL AROUND THE WORLD

J O S H U A   A R A N D T

This was inspired by a chance meeting with a man who befriended me in a café. He was being treated at a clinic nearby and told me he was getting out for a breath of fresh air.

'You want to know shit I can tell you shit 32 years of *shit* man poverty torture manipulation substance abuse physical abuse in and out of institutions of schools and hospitals and takeaway joints all types of *shit* man but I'm staying positive look see these tears here yeah the ones tattooed on my cheek well they're tears of hope and on my arm here these little holes are from the injections though I say *FUCK THAT I DON'T WANT SO MANY, WHY DON'T YOU GIVE ME HALF THAT* and so they give me these pills instead which turn me into a fucking six-inch dwarf wouldn't even be able to ride the Tea Cups at Disneyland a tiny shadow of myself so fuck it those go in the bin now and when I get sad I just sing in my little death-metal voice like this ERRGGHHHHHGGHHHGH but I spend more time at this café than I do next door in the wards so maybe I should just consider myself an in-patient of sub-standard lattes of crusty focaccias instead though if I'm honest none of it started with cafés or food or anything like that though I'm a chef by trade no it started with my mum but not in that leave-you-locked-up-in-the-car-while-I-piss-away-everything-on-the-pokies sort of way but in a trippy way bro I saw her in a Morbid Angel clip on Rage one morning and it went on for like twenty seconds she was wearing this amazing dress all floral like and crying as if someone had died and so I got really scared thinking I was about to die and when I told my brother he fucking turned on me my own flesh and blood and so we all went down to JB and bought the tape and watched it but she wasn't on it no more and the next minute they're taking me into some clinic telling me to keep my shit together and I'm telling them *I'm a fucking pacifist man, I wouldn't hurt a fly* and when they realise I'm telling the truth they just leave me alone which is even more degrading I used to be a big thing in the music industry 17 years down there in Melbourne town way into the underground scene dub and reggae mixed in with metal and a tiny bit of funk and electro you know that sort of sound a-bounca bounca boomp and I was doing this gig at the Espy the first time they came for me pulled me right off the stage though when I look back it was probably a good thing as there's no fucking money in that business and if you don't have money you don't have food and if you don't have food you don't have anything to eat see I'm a chef by trade so that's my purpose grow food go organic educate people in the community live local think global all that sort of shit there's a lot of people up here interested in sustainability and I sit on some local board so I can lobby against big city bankers and lawyer types that eat too much just eat and eat and eat gorge themselves on injected cows and pedicured lawns with pop-up sprinklers and when I tell them I want to start something here something local when I say I want the *tiniest* fucking wall around the town they look down through their crème brulee covered snouts and think *I'm the crazy one* grab me by the shoulders and say *Here have some lawn seed, spatter a little of this on you, grow up nice and green and shiny so we can come round with clippers trim back the edges,* and OK I'll admit to occasionally talking to Snoop Dog and Vladimir Putin or more that Putin talks to me and maybe *just maybe* I should keep that shit to myself but does that mean everything I say's completely useless I got this mate see who was bitten by three snakes on the way to the pub one afternoon and I was like *How the fuck do you get bitten by three fucking snakes when all you're doing is walking to the pub* and he's like *I don't know man I was just walking down the street and I got bitten by three snakes and now all I fucking see is snakes, snakes with my eyes open, snakes with my eyes shut* and you know what they do to this man they give him shock-fucking-therapy this dude's channeling some deep shit could be a shaman or witchdoctor a man of great responsibility and they just hole him up in that white walled fucking porta-loo over there pump him full of drugs and disinfectant and stick his brain in a giant toaster wheel him in and out in a chair like he's eighty-fucking-six they tried that shit with me man tried to wheel me in and out and I said *GET OUT OF IT I CAN WALK THANK-YOU-VERY-MUCH I'VE GOT TWO LEGS HAVEN'T I* and when they realise I'm harmless they pay me even less attention eyes glaze over like somebody's mixed flour through them glaze the way they do when I go on about Putin and how he comes across as a prick though he's really soft as shit you know if Putin came up right now and said he wanted to wrestle then we'd fucking wrestle I'd grab him in a lung-choke and say *Hey man I learned this shit from my Chinese brothers* channel some major Bruce Lee shit and afterwards I've give him a little bit of a tickle and say *You want to do this, you really want to do this* but he's a big fucking sook that Vladimir he'd just say *No no* and I'd say *Then settle the fuck down would ya, settle the FUCK down and stop trying to seem so hard, go grab yourself a focaccia, go hang out with Gina Vaginahert and sell shit to Asia, if you have to start building walls, build a big fucking wall around the whole world, keep us safe from anyone who's floating down from outer space* but they don't understand man get in the chair they say wheel me in wheel me out all day long

in and out
in and out.'

DETERMINATION

DETERMINATION

Photos by Bess Meredith

THROUGH THE FOG

B E S S   M E R E D I T H

> *As you learn to love and respect yourself, and accept that depression is there—you can believe that you can fight it. Through this new awareness, I am stitching myself back together. Perhaps each time I do this, it is with a stronger thread, so it'll be harder for it to ever come undone again.*

The worst days are when you feel so sad that it hurts to smile. I struggle to speak, to remember words; the sky feels too bright and my eyes want to shut it all away. I find myself looking blankly at a child's face—so young, all they want is my attention, a smile—and my heart aches as my face tries to paint one on.

For much of my 20s I've lived with the mindset, 'If I could just study this, travel there, get a job in this, a house here, a husband/wife at this time …then I will be happy!' I think many of us live like this to some extent, because it is important to dream and make plans. But every time I would try to commit to these dreams and make changes in my life, I kept falling down. At times I was paralysed by fear, unable to leave the house; other days I would end up sobbing in bed, unable to pull myself out of it. I would tell myself this was ridiculous, pathetic. This was the darkness that entered my mind and made life seem too hard, too bleak, pointless. This was the burden of depression.

Recently I found a notepad from a time when I had decided to limit my food intake and write everything down. Three carrots, five almonds, one piece of bread. I guess I thought if I could control at least one aspect of my life things might return to normal. But, of course, reducing my intake of food made me even less rational, and when I failed in eating such unfair portions, the guilt and sense of failure I felt only fuelled my absolute hate of myself and reinforced the self negativity: 'You really are a stupid, worthless, pathetic. Nobody likes your art, nobody likes you. You are not lovable and therefore you don't deserve to exist.' A rational mind can challenge all this negative and paranoid thinking, it can see how unrealistic and even silly it is; a depressed mind cannot. It is so far down, so full of horrible little voices that it can't be lifted up.

The incessant taunting of suicidal thoughts frightened me at first, as I knew they were abnormal and I tried my best to suppress them, to rationalise them—but this only made them stronger and in turn made me more anxious. I began to have anxiety attacks. When I sat in lectures at university I could not focus—words and images would blur, and I would try to slow my racing mind to concentrate, but it would always wander back to thoughts of my own death. My heart would race, my would skin prickle, and

I would rush from the room gasping for breath. I would have to leave school because I was unable to deal with talking to anyone, so I would go home to bed. I felt I had lost complete control of my mind, and that there was no way back. I was incredibly ashamed that I could not regulate my thoughts or feelings. I would cry for seemingly no reason, and I could not cope in what should have been simple situations. I came to believe that the only way to calm all of this chaos in my head would be to die.

Depression is a very hard thing to carry alone, and for a long time I tried to protect those around me from it. I didn't tell many people about the first time I went on anti-depressants, just the doctor I was getting them from. And I remember being too afraid even to tell him that the only relief I was getting was in daydreams of my own death. I felt trapped in trying to spare the worry of my loved ones, and trapped in the fear of what people would think of me. I was scared they would put me in the psych ward. I was scared of being defined by my depression, and labelled as either 'crazy' or 'lazy'. This stigma was enough to keep me quiet and trying to keep living a life that matched up to what I thought were everyone's expectations of me. Of course I would never put these expectations on a stranger or loved one, so why did I do it to myself for so long? I ached for relief from my own head, wishing someone would just tell me, 'Bess, you need to be in hospital'.

I did end up in hospital. One Sunday morning I couldn't get out of bed. I woke up anxious and lay there trying to decide what to do when I got up. The anxiety had so completely taken over my mind that I felt overwhelmed by the smallest decisions. I couldn't decide whether to get up and eat or shower first. This literally kept me in bed and then the shame I started to feel at not being able to make this simple, seemingly stupid decision to just get up made me cry and I just couldn't stop. And the thoughts of self-loathing set in as I asked myself, 'How pathetic is it that you can't even get up out of bed?' The negative thoughts went round and round and the pain was so intense that I thrashed my head against the wall in an effort to stop the pain inside.

I was meant to go and see a show with my parents, but I texted them to say I couldn't make it. I knew things were not right in my head. I thought of two close friends I could call. I didn't feel safe. But I was ashamed and couldn't make the call.

Sometime in the afternoon I managed to get up and have a glass of wine with my housemate. It wasn't a good idea; after she went to bed I couldn't stop. I'd had some Valium, and started feeling even further disconnected from myself. And then I just thought, 'How long can I be trapped in this endless cycle? When will this pain ever stop? What's the point?' It was all suddenly so loud in my head and I longed for reprieve.

I rummaged through my medicines. I managed to get down forty Panadol, forty anti-depressants and maybe ten Valium. I was so scared. I cried. But at the time, I could see no other option.

It is the most awful fate to lose control over one's own mind.

Nothing could make you feel less alive, less human, than the nothing that you feel.

You are no longer here, and yet you are nowhere else.

A complete disconnect.

I awoke the next day and realised what I had done. My housemate found me and called my dad to take me to the hospital. I had to stay on a drip for 24 hours to reverse the effects of the drugs so my liver would survive, so I would survive. I was deeply embarrassed and ashamed. But it was a relief to be in hospital. I had cracked—all the pain and hardship I had been carrying in every fibre of my being had finally spilled out. Release. For the first time in a long, long time, I felt safe from the depression, from the dangers of myself.

Some people try to commit suicide and, in recovery, they deeply regret ever attempting it; they have an epiphany to go on living. When I was in the hospital I can't say I was relieved to be alive, but I saw the tortured faces of my loved ones and, of course, told the doctors and nurses that I would never try it again. At the time though I don't think I had any idea of how I really felt. I was not dead—but I was not quite mentally back from the darkness. I feel like no one could ever explain how hard it is trying to emerge from the other side of that. You're supposed to feel grateful you survived, but you are also not sure how to move forward. It feels harrowing, and lonely.

For many years I had longed to have an explainable physical illness—a neat explanation for the fatigue, the anxiety, for the fact that my friends never saw me anymore. The ironic part is that for me depression is a very physical experience: my blood feels like syrup, slowly moving through my veins. I struggle to move, to talk—everything feels like an effort, and I just want to stay in bed. But how could I try to explain that these feelings, physical as well as mental, were the effects of a real illness? Part of why it has taken me so long to learn how to manage my depression is because of my own lack of acceptance and a lack of acknowledgment of its existence. But the more you try to ignore the depression or push it away, the stronger it becomes, until it consumes every part of your being.

When you have nothing to compare your thoughts with, it can be hard to recognise them as unhealthy. It's easy to assume that you are a weak person, that there is something fundamentally flawed in your being; you're just too sensitive for this world. But through treatment I have learnt that worry, low self-esteem, negativity, despair, physical self-harm, an overwhelming lack of emotional control and thoughts of suicide are not something that everyone experiences regularly, or should be experiencing regularly. I have spent many years trying to work on this, and have realised that self-protection is key. As you learn to love and respect yourself, and accept that depression is there, you can believe that you can fight it. Through this new awareness, I am stitching myself back together. Perhaps each time I do this, it is with a stronger thread, so it'll be harder for it to ever come undone again.

Another sufferer once said to me, 'Hey, it's only part of who we are, not all of who we are and I reckon we're pretty great!' And I think this is a really important distinction to make. While depression at times consumes us, it isn't all of us. But we cannot deny its presence. Remaining silent about what we are experiencing does nothing to help us.

I've had three major episodes of depression, the latest being the most confronting. Recently my mum said, 'You are becoming more and more yourself again in these last couple of weeks.' And sometimes its not until you hear this, that you realise you really did disappear for a while. If you have depression, at some point you are forced to stop, to reassess, to confront. It is only then that we can see clearly who we are, and who is by our side. And working our way through the dark, painful experience, we start to appreciate the little things, the small triumphs: managing a walk outside, looking up at the sky, the trees, watching a lizard bathing in the sun.

Recovery is slow,

but feelings—often overwhelmingly—begin to return

and gradually,

the fog starts to lift.

ALIVE AT WILLIAMSTOWN PIER

adapted from excerpts of the play by

N E I L   C O L E

ACT I, SCENE I

Williamstown has four piers. The first is strategically placed between the ice-cream shop and the fish and chip shop. When you've finished your fish and chips, you can buy an ice-cream, then walk onto the pier and gaze at the city and its tall buildings.

NEIL:
The night I swept the pier I bought a broom from the Williamstown hardware shop and swept and swept and swept. It took all night. I started to hear strange voices and see strange things. That's when I really knew something was wrong.

ACT I, SCENE 2

Neil's home, devoid of any furniture.

NEIL:
In my manic phase, my days passed with the consistency of a hurricane. It's amazing what you can do in a 22-hour waking day. Amazing what you look like on a 22-hour day. I still didn't have enough time to get everything done, so I went faster and faster. I swam faster at the pool—so much faster that my times were almost of Olympic standard. I tore some muscles, because the speed that my mind wanted me to go was faster than my body could go. I also got rid of all the furniture in my house, keeping only a bed and a bean bag. I cleaned my bathroom every day and sometimes more—seven times one night was the record. I still didn't have enough time to get everything done, so I went even faster and faster and got less and less done or so it seemed.

ACT I, SCENE 3

The pier, again.

NEIL:
In my melancholic phase I thought of coming to the pier. It didn't make me feel better, but it didn't make me feel worse. There were even times when I found myself on the pier, looking at waves hitting pylons, and only then realising how depressed I actually was. One thing mania did was give me less time to be depressed. When my mania was under reasonable control I had so much more time to resonate on my depression. With my depression, however, came the paradox of my relationship with my two little boys. When they weren't with me I'd miss them and when I was with them I couldn't cope. I'd substitute the latest toy I couldn't afford for the love I didn't think I could give. I'd stand on the pier with them, gazing blankly into mid-air. Something was very wrong, they knew, not because of this but because I was the only one without an ice-cream. We'd look at the big cargo ships, their awesome slow movement enough to frighten any small boy, and me. In time I will stand here aware of them, without depression, and know I am finally alive at Williamstown pier.

DOUG COX

interview by

C O N O R   H U T C H I S O N

---

*It struck me that Doug had yet again managed to recover
from a significant setback, to find strength and resilience
in the face of all his adversity.*

Doug Cox is a former VFL player, sprinter, football coach, and successful businessman. He is also a long-standing sufferer of depression and anxiety. Doug works with Children of Parents with a Mental Illness (COPMI) and is committed to helping improve the situation for others. But it was a different story for Doug, who before the age of 35 had never sought treatment for his own mental health problems. He had to also approach the problem of raising a young family while managing his mental health issues at a time when there was little support and widespread stigma. It put an awful strain on Doug's personal relationships, especially with his four daughters, three of whom still refuse to talk to him. For Doug, telling his story is a way to help others and a way to hopefully open up the lines of communication with his daughters again.

GROWING UP AND RUNNING AWAY

Doug was born in Mildura and lived there until his mid-teens. In 1971, when he was 14, his three eldest siblings moved on and his parents split. A week later his brother committed suicide. Doug and his younger sister were sent to Sydney to live with their mother. Two years later, when Doug finished year 10, his mother remarried and he chose to move out.

'I can't blame her for my illness,' Doug said, 'but she certainly had a part in it. She was very cruel, very self-absorbed. When you were around her, all the love went to her.'

He saw his mother less than a dozen times after that. Doug ran away from his older sister's place and back to Mildura when he was 17. 'I really had no direction. I was very naive, very scared and very insecure'. In an attempt to find direction Doug joined the Army and did clerical work. He developed self-discipline—an attribute that would later help him through gruelling sports training—and had a successful working life. But he was still unable to develop a sense of belonging.

'You're all over the place. Posted here, posted there. Then with football you go from here, go to there. Life's taken me to a lot of different places.'

Doug relocated back to Sydney and then on to Adelaide where he began playing Australian Rules Football in the evenings. He was soon picked to play for South Australia and after a year was spotted by a talent scout of the St Kilda Football Club. But with an Army contract keeping him in Adelaide he was forced to decline. The problem was rectified by the president of the club, Lindsay Fox. 'Lindsay knew quite a lot of people. He made it happen. Two weeks later I was in Melbourne.'

FOOTBALL

The signing with St Kilda became controversial when Richmond realised that, according to zoning rules, Doug was legally their player. Doug was in the newspapers as 'the man at the centre of one of the VFL's most controversial clearance disputes'. St Kilda lost all their premiership points and the clubs had to resolve the issue on the steps of the Supreme court with Richmond offering to officially hand Doug over to St Kilda for $80,000. However, Doug's hardship was largely ignored in the shadow of the club's potential demise.

'I had a horrific time while all that was going on. I just had no idea what was happening to me and what was happening around. I had become very suicidal and withdrawn, with no one to turn to.'

After the trial Doug went on to play the rest of the season but continued to experience volatile mood swings. He had extreme highs and extreme lows and nothing in between. Doug's performance on the field was also dependent on how he was feeling on game day.

That season and most of the next one were highly successful until St Kilda fell into financial trouble and couldn't afford to pay their players. Doug had just married and needed a steady income, and when he approached the general manager about the issue it turned into an argument. Doug quit the club. The commotion was overheard by someone from the office who alerted the newspapers and when Doug arrived home he was bombarded with phone calls. One reporter, who Doug knew fairly well, asked him to explain what had happened 'off the record' and Doug obliged. He woke up to read the headline 'Cox quits and calls admin bunglers'. The club rang him and said, 'You'll never play football again.' His anxiety and panic attacks continued, his suicidal thoughts intensified.

Even though Doug's mental health was affecting him both on and off the field, he was still considered a valuable player after leaving St Kilda. He was asked to play for a couple of clubs, but when Kevin Sheedy of Essendon came to Doug's house, he signed. Doug managed to have a good amount of game play despite injuries. Winning the 1983 VFL Reserves Grand Final with Essendon against Collingwood was a highlight, as was running first in the 1984 Grand Final Sprint.

In 1985 he moved with his wife to Adelaide so she could be close to her parents. He was not able to pay back the faith that Essendon had in him and eventually the guilt began to plague his thoughts. His mental illness still untreated, Doug became deeply depressed. He and his wife separated and he left Adelaide for a coaching job with a country football club for a year. On his return, he met his second wife and the new relationship inspired him to make a comeback to football with West Torrens for one more season. They had two daughters during this time and moved up north.

'We used to go camping or fishing, which they loved. My wife's family were very close and we would have a BBQ every Sunday. I really enjoyed this as my family were the complete opposite.'

In Brisbane Doug briefly worked as a fitness trainer but his own lack of fitness made it difficult to train at the level required. The lack of sport also contributed to his worst episode yet.

'One morning my wife woke up and I'm naked and lying on the floor, shaking, in the foetal position, and had no idea where I was or what I was doing or what was wrong with me. That is when I went to the doctor and received the first diagnosis and started a very long journey trying to get the right diagnosis and the right treatment.'

The shock of going to a doctor was quickly followed by relief. 'I had finally found out the name of the feelings I had been experiencing all my life: anxiety, panic and depression.' Looking back, Doug was glad he had not asked for help during his sporting career for fear of how the club and supporters would have reacted.

BUSINESS

At 35, his sports career behind him, and finally engaging in treatment for his mental health, Doug refocused. During the first round of interviews for a position at one of the biggest electrical companies in Australia, he discovered the advantages of his football fame. The employment consultant was a football fan from Melbourne and assured Doug that he would make it to the next round. At the next stage Doug was lucky again—the CEO fondly recalled how he used to watch Doug's AFL games as a kid. When the state manager preferred another candidate, the CEO told him it was Doug or no one. The CEO's faith in Doug was repaid and twelve months after getting the job he was asked to replace the state manager and rebuild the company. Doug hired new agents and merchandisers and increased the company's annual profit significantly. He attributed his success to the way he treated the buyers and customers.

'I didn't treat my customers as customers; I treated them as business partners. We worked together to build each other's businesses and we would do anything and everything to make sure that happened. I built a lot of trust.'

Despite new-found success, his mental health remained unstable. After one year as state manager he returned to hospital—Doug would spend more than three years on and off in psychiatric wards. Doug associated his first experiences in wards with an 'overwhelming feeling of fear and being alone', but after more visits he began to think of them as a safe place. For one particularly bad episode he was required to stay in hospital for six weeks. A couple of the buyers had experienced depression, so when he let them know about his own mental health issues they were happy to take on some of his tasks. The CEO provided support to Doug and his family and continued to pay him his full salary. They even began having sales meetings in the psychiatric ward. The buyers would arrive and find an empty room and sit together with Doug as though they were having a regular meeting. Later, the periods spent in the psychiatric wards, away from his family and his regular life, were increasingly difficult. Doug continued working at the electrical company for three years until the company was restructured and he was made redundant.

But Doug wasn't always able to successfully balance his life and his mental health. After the electrical company he found another job with a well-known small appliances company, but the time away from his family in the psychiatric wards had began to put pressure on his marriage.

'My second wife had enough of—well, she'd had enough of it all—I tried to commit suicide and, I mean, I was in hospital and she'd just had enough. She just came up and said, "Look, don't come home."'

His second wife filed for divorce and Doug made steps to again rebuild his life. He began working again, this time in the flooring industry, where he stayed for many years. After increasing the company's profit from $30,000 to $100,000 a month, he bought a flooring franchise. He then bought a house and moved in with his new girlfriend. But his mental health problems continued and he went back into hospital and hired new staff to take over his job. However, the same level of support Doug had received at the electrical company was not available with his new career and the budget began to slip.

'When you're not there, you don't have that control and they kept it from me. They didn't tell me how bad things were getting, so it was a bit of a shock when I came out and I was told the extent of the damage.'

By the time Doug left hospital, the franchise had gone under and he had lost his house. Soon afterwards, his relationship with his girlfriend also broke down.

OLD FRIENDS AND NEW BEGINNINGS

The next three years of Doug's life were very dark. It is difficult for him to talk about this time, not only because of painful memories but also because of the absence of memories.

'I really lost the plot and I bought a motorbike and I just started to ride and took off and I became very self-destructive and self-harmed a lot. I remember I actually rode out to Uluru and I worked out there and I don't remember it … I got really foggy for about two or three years.'

This dark period ended when he moved to Adelaide—two of Doug's school friends, Paul and Jeff, and Paul's wife Josie, helped him through.

'When I was in the Army over in Adelaide, the three of us lived together. Paul was at Uni. Jeff was working at Ansett back in those days. And we've just remained very, very close. The two boys ring me all the time now.'

In the months following our interview, Doug and I kept in contact and exchanged ideas on the piece. However, in late February there was no reply and I grew worried. A few weeks later a reply came and he apologised, explaining that he was recovering from a heart attack but that his health was good. It struck me that Doug had yet again managed to recover from a significant setback, to find strength and resilience in the face of all his adversity. It is the major theme of his story—Doug's desire to understand his problems, to help others through his work at the COPMI, and to attempt to reconnect with his family.

One in three people in Australia will have a mental illness or know someone close to them who does. Without people who are willing to tell their story, such as Doug, the stigma will continue to overshadow the lived experience of people with mental illness and prevent them from seeking help. Doug and his family's lives would have been very different if, when Doug had initially asked for help from his family doctor, his GP had recognised the relevance of family to an individual's mental health. Doug's relationship with his mother and the suicide of his brother contributed to his mental illness, and now as a parent, his mental illness is affecting his relationships with his children. Although mental health services are beginning to recognise the relevance of family to mental health, it is important for people like Doug to continue to advocate for better mental health awareness and improve support for families.

Report

by a psych nurse at a hospital

An Australian male, from a middle class family. He lives in a bungalow out the back and has a history of poor performance at school. Not sporty either. Has a few good friends, but has trouble getting and keeping girlfriends and work. He weighs 150 kg and is covered in tattoos, poor self-esteem. Recently has been withdrawing from his family. He has been on the anti-depressant Xanax, which is very addictive, and doesn't work for everyone. Last week he took an OD of Xanax and texted some friends, who rang his parents and an ambulance. So, cry for help rather than serious attempt to end his life. He was combative towards the ambulance officers and police were also called so he could be subdued with intra-muscular sedation. Once he was deposited in the emergency dept he again was combative. The staff had no alternative but to call a Code Grey (where security and orderlies attend to hold a patient down so they can either be restrained or sedated or both). This young man was so strong that the medical staff had to knock him completely out with sedatives, which meant that they had to place a breathing tube down his throat and ventilate him. Thus he visits me in Intensive Care. Because he has a history of amphetamine and ecstasy use he is quite resistant to our drugs, requiring large doses. He remains with us for five days, acquiring a chest infection in the process. He is so strong and aggressive that careful plans are put in place with psychiatrists and the code grey team for when he is weaned off the sedation and ventilator. I last saw him a few nights back, breathing on his own, but not cooperative and thus restrained in the bed. The psychiatrist will most likely admit him to the psych unit for counselling and a review of his anti-depressants. Then his poor family have to pick up the pieces.

With the benefit of hindsight I wonder if it would have been better just to have a medical person observe him at home while he slept off the effects of the Xanax, and then for the psychs to step in. He didn't need all that medical intervention for a deteriorating state, but only because he was combative. He was only combative because he was in our environment. Intensive care beds are in short supply and expensive. It was very traumatic for his family to witness their son being restrained, chemically and physically. This young man is only 27 years old, and this first OD often leads to a pattern of repetitive behaviour, draining everyone's resources. He has a history of joining bikie gangs, but not fitting in (again) and being kicked out. It seems to me the most important thing for these depressed people is to fit in. I wonder how much psych counselling is put in to finding the right niche for these troubled people so they can gain some self respect. Not enough I suspect. It is easier just to prescribe 'different' drugs and make an appointment for a month's time.

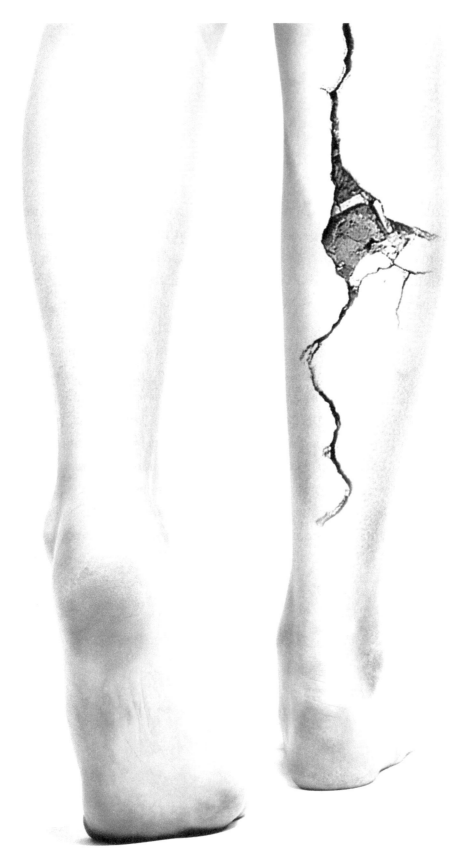

RECOVERY ROAD

K A T H   C O U R T S

What's it like to live with an eating disorder?
It's excruciating

I had tonsillitis and I wasn't hungry. Fast forward a few months and I found myself living with an eating disorder.

I heard a punitive voice that told me I wasn't allowed to eat, that I didn't need to eat, that I was weak for thinking I should eat something. It was all or nothing and I quickly felt powerless over the voice of the eating disorder guiding me to nothingness.

Living out of home, and with no voice of reason in my life, my eating disorder became a parent of sorts. It was a voice of discipline, control and perfection. I had to be good and do what I was told—my eating disorder was soothing on a 'good day' and punishing when I 'failed'.

My days became completely tied up in thoughts and behaviours around food. I joined the gym and felt strong—I thought I was taking control of my health and was determined to lose weight and prove that I could do it. It was a distraction from my grief and worries about family relationships that were pretty unpleasant.

I went to university and didn't enjoy my classes. I struggled to concentrate and felt different to other people. They seemed to laugh and have loud conversations as I sat on my own, hesitant and increasingly isolated. Eventually I withdrew from my studies, it was a waste of time and I could only think of ways to ensure I didn't have to eat.

What's it like to live with an eating disorder?

It's excruciating.

I moved in with my sister and my eating disorder intensified. I slept as long as I could and when I woke up I moved to the sofa to watch TV and I refused to go into the kitchen. I knew that I was tempting fate to open the fridge, the voice in my head told me that I hadn't done anything energetic so the food would just turn to fat, and this frightened me. My mind was so full of fear so much of the time that I was exhausted. It's strange to remember that time now, I can see the lies that I was telling myself. It's shocking to realise how consumed I was by my eating disorder and how resigned I was to a future with it.

I didn't pretend to be OK, my sister knew I wasn't well, and I seemed to either be confident that I could live without food or so overwhelmingly terrified that I was about to die that I felt incapacitated until I regained my misguided strength. During the day

I pushed myself to exercise and limit my food intake and at the end of the day I was relieved I had got through it, and dreaded the day to follow. I felt suicidal but didn't want to be found dead and fat so I kept waking up and being controlled by my eating disorder.

I became a different person. I was paranoid and angry, and spent more time alone. I was desperate to sleep more and avoid life.

At a certain point I found myself at an assessment for an inpatient stay in hospital. I had become so weak and so mentally vulnerable that I agreed to go and try to find help. I was really scared and I didn't really think it would fix me, but I went along with it and ended up in hospital a few weeks later.

It was awful. I was given food to eat, and I had no choice but to eat it. I felt like I was crawling out of my skin and I stopped getting dressed, hanging out in my pyjamas because I didn't see the point. The difficult part of having an eating disorder—the pain, confusion and frustration—is that my eating disorder didn't want me to get better, and so I believed I didn't want to get better. I believed that voice that told me I didn't want to relax around food, I didn't want to eat normally, I didn't want to challenge my thoughts. I felt that recovery would leave me on my own and I didn't know what life would be like without it.

After some time in hospital I started to feel better, it was still a challenge to eat adequately and I rarely felt comfortable in myself but I knew that I could recover and I wanted to get better and live again. The hospital stay meant I had some time out from my life and I had time to consider what I wanted and I finally allowed myself to believe that I didn't want to live with an eating disorder but I wanted to experience joy and friendship and opportunity again.

What's it like to be in recovery from an eating disorder?

At first I felt overwhelmed that I had survived and I wanted to go and do all these things I had never done before. I looked at courses, investigated work options, and planned for the future. I hadn't allowed myself to look forward or hope for anything, so the excitement was huge and I didn't know where to start.

I was still very conscious of food—what I was eating and what others were eating. I wanted to be well but I didn't know how it would work and so I found myself stopping short of completely challenging the fears and concerns I had around food. I was relieved to feel better, but I couldn't believe it would last.

It got easier, people told me I looked well and I didn't recoil. I was proud of what I'd achieved and I wanted others to know that recovery is possible. I don't know that I enjoyed eating, but I became able to be spontaneous and to try new things and to practise being at peace with my body so that it didn't cause me so much anxiety.

When I searched for eating disorders online, looking for support, I came across The Butterfly Foundation. Their website told me they were a charity who offered support to those going through an eating disorder and I couldn't read it fast enough. I searched through all the pages to find as much as I could about what they had to offer and I sent them an email. I found it too hard to make the phone call but I wanted to know that I could get better.

I heard from a counsellor and it was an incredible support. I'd always known that I was the only one who could make the choice to eat and follow my meal plan. But Butterfly helped me to feel safe to make that choice. Using their support alongside my own team meant that whether I was with friends, in a session, or at home I had someone I could talk to in a difficult moment.

I went to college and completed a Bachelor's degree and I managed to do really well rather than struggle through. I made new friends and was involved in social activities and I felt satisfied. Food wasn't the be all and end all of my world any more.

But, and here's where it gets difficult, my eating disorder was a reaction to trauma and events from my past that I hadn't processed and recovered from. As I recovered, I did find more energy and positive attitude, but the triggers for the illness had not been dealt with and so it lurked in the back of my mind. Whenever I became stressed or overwhelmed, I retreated into the comfort of the illness. It sounds really weird to say it was comfortable, or safe, because an eating disorder is neither of those things, and yet I felt seduced by the voice telling me that if I just ate a particular way, and weighed a particular amount, I would have order and nothing could catch me off guard.

So when I went through a difficult time, I found that I needed to plan my meals and focus my attention. I didn't like the feeling of anxiety and panic and sadness I felt in the face of family drama and I knew I didn't want to be ill, but I knew I would feel better for a little while if I managed my diet a little better. And a little better turned into a little more, and then more. And I relapsed.

What's it like to relapse?

I'd get dressed and hope no one noticed I didn't have the energy to shower that day. I had some cereal, and it hurt. I didn't want to do it. But I knew I had to. I knew I couldn't trust myself. There's a voice, that sounds so much like me, saying 'It's too sweet, I don't like it, I'm not hungry …' And when it's done I can feel my skin bubbling and resenting my actions. It's like acid causing angry blisters.

I continued to live my life. To the outside world I was happy—people told me I looked well, I'd go to work and meet with friends and look forward to the weekend like normal people do. But I had to find the time to walk, to force my feet to the ground.

I am marching, without joy, only fear and control urging me to keep going. I am weighing out my food and hoping that no one catches me, no desire, only fear and control demanding that I stick to the rules. I am eating at set times in my day and refusing to listen to the ache in my chest, no respect for myself, only fear and control.

My sister would hug me with caution, joking that my bones hurt her. My mum stepped in and said she was worried. My psychologist challenged my truths, she kept telling me I couldn't go on this way. My eating disorder was growing stronger by the day and I heard the voice in my head laugh because my psychologist was wrong. *I can go on this way and I will go on this way.*

Until one night I found myself crying, and I realised that this wasn't the way it was meant to be. I'd known happy days and good times and connections with friends and that is what I wanted. I didn't want to wake up another day to monotony and agony. I allowed myself to acknowledge that I had a choice and I could recover again. I needed to talk to someone and I found myself logging on to Butterfly's webchat. I was so overwhelmed with panic and I felt really out of control. I wanted someone to be able to hear what I was saying and not tell me that I just needed to eat more and it would get better. I knew the counsellor I spoke to would understand, not ask me to do anything but be there. And so I logged on and I typed and typed and got it all out. And I felt better.

I logged on again the next day. I spoke to someone different and found the same result. When I shared how I was feeling, the counsellor asked me what the healthy part of me was thinking and suddenly I reconnected. When the panic set in I was in no state to be rational or logical in my approach and the whole idea of recovery seemed out of reach. After a chat with a counsellor I suddenly remembered who I was, who I wanted to be and what I was fighting for. And it was a fight that I suddenly had hope of winning.

Recovery road

I made the choice and I started to eat. And it was small steps, hesitant choices, an incredible amount of love, patience and support from my family, my friends and my treatment team. An eating disorder is a loud, vindictive, angry and malevolent identity. I found that, for me, her power diminished every time someone spoke my name and asked me what I wanted. A simple act of kindness, rubbing my feet or telling me I was worth the meal in front of me, appealing to the healthy part of me that so desperately wanted to be better and stronger. Love is powerful.

I've found that my recovery doesn't go in a straight line and the dreams I had of waking without an eating disorder to greet me have not come true. But I have hope that, in time, my body and my mind will get used to being well, and instead of trying to break negative habits, I will find a natural instinct that exists within me to nourish my body and respect myself.

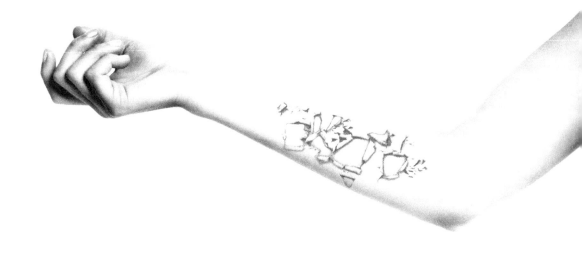

THE PINEAL GLAND

Z O E   B L A I N

Yoga class eight pm

There's a leg wrapped round

your neck and you can't Zen-out

'cause a poster of the cardiovascular system

is staring straight at you.

Miniature nuclear explosions

run up the body's centre

a flash on the forehead

THIRD EYE

and your instructor, over chanting

is saying something about the pineal gland

the soul and transcendence.

When you tasted the chemical tang of your first anti-depressant

the carving 'SSRI' was like a hieroglyph of ancient Egypt

(you were the tourist).

Through psychology's infatuation with neuroscience

you learned the language of the synapse.

If you drilled a hole through the skull

and peered in with a strong pair of binoculars

you might acquaint yourself with five hundred trillion synapses.

Imagine two fingertips nearly touching:

one tip holding keys (serotonin)

the other locks.

This is the synapse.

When serotonin wants to make a statement

it crosses the gap and with a twist

click and

swing

electric waves excite central nervous system firings.

When intercourse is over

the key slips from the lock and

slinks back to its residential fingers. This is reuptake and SSRIs won't allow it

serotonin jamming halfway in for precise mood stabilisation.

Psychology class eleven am.

You're on twenty milligrams of Escitalopram Oxalate

and René Descartes sits

sketching diagrams of the brain beside you.

'Hey Zo, do you think the pineal could be the seat of the soul?

The point where consciousness docks to the physical body?'

You smile vaguely,

picturing Michelangelo's *Creation of Adam*.

Can René feel his thoughts trickling

out of the abstract and down

through his spinal fluid

(the body's own Amazon river)

electrifying the tips of his fingers as they grip the nib and scribble?

When you finally kicked your serotonin habit

you had head pains, gut aches and

squabbling intestines.

But it was the dreams

the stupid

VIVID

dreams

that warped you the hardest.

The pineal gland,

an intimate venue located on the spinal cord's top rung

hosts the biggest serotonin conference in the human body.

Blood

is sent straight up from the heart for refreshments.

The pineal is also a factory where

hair-netted workers transform serotonin into melatonin

the brain's naturally occurring sleeping tablet;

its defence against tumours and

chemical abnormalities.

In the twentieth century a rumour was started

about a secret pineal office

where chemists synthesised and stashed large DMT doses.

Dimethyltryptamine: the most renowned and pious psychedelic chemical

a blueprint for dreams, hallucinations and

near death experiences.

DMT. A specialist locksmith

who can crack serotonin's exclusive keyholes.

When you smoke DMT

your limbs pack up like a jigsaw puzzle

your eyes turn solid twenty-four carat gold.

You might be pawning them at the local shopping centre

when you realise you don't have a body.

A shopper in a lab coat advises:

'Keep those eyeballs, you might need 'em later.

Don't sell your pineal either.'

He mumbles something about pathologists

finding DMT in the pineals of corpses.

The floor starts splitting;

a chasm of DNA chains, serpents and celestial bodies.

Lab Coat pulls a diagram out of his breast pocket.

It maps DMT, serotonin and melatonin's molecular structures.

Branches and leaves... it's a family tree

'cause they've all got the same ancestors.

Suddenly his hands are your hands and they're heavy.

The last thing you remember

is that the trip was mighty familiar,

quite similar

to all those weird, vivid dreams you've been having.

The twentieth century stripped the soul from its seat and

labelled Descartes archaic and mystic.

The pineals of most western citizens

calcify during their second decade of living;

the factory hit by a sudden recession

weathering into the sand of a cool, lonely beach

where you sit,

building castles of chemicals

tossing SSRIs into the ocean

dreaming

deep

and considering everything.

TRUE NORTH

CHRIS WALPOLE

I guess people don't really understand how it affects you. There is the word depression, people take that on but they don't really ask what that means. Depths of despair is how I would put it. Some people just think 'oh just snap out of it, you'll be right' but you just can't. I think depression can affect anyone, from any walk of life.

I went and did some travels in my car. Just my dog and I went across the deserts. In a way, I was searching for something. I was just trying to find out what was going on under the surface. My surface. I had an adventurous spirit in a way but I'd never talked about depression. Depression sat beside me the whole way.

My upbringing made me feel we men shouldn't feel this way. Unsure. Sad. Being a parent now with my son, I talk to him about the way that he feels, that it's important, and that it is OK to feel the way that he does. We have a really good relationship—we hug a lot, we are very affectionate and talk a lot about stuff. We talk about how he is feeling: 'what upsets you?', 'how does that make you feel?', 'are you OK about that?' I think it has made me a better parent in that way. My kids are very wise, Karah and Lachlan, their heads are on their shoulders. They are happy and they are well-rounded. They are old souls. They appreciate things in life. If you give them something they really appreciate it. It doesn't have to be the latest gadget, it can be something simple and they will appreciate it. I talk to my kids about mental illness and how it can affect people. They know that I take medication and I see a psychologist. They are OK with it. They are supportive. I never got any of that as a kid. It was always so busy at home. I had five brothers and sisters growing up with me, so I felt lost and I wanted attention but I didn't know how to ask for it. Kids don't.

I am good with people and I am good at understanding and at showing empathy. I like doing that, making people feel good about themselves. Trying to offer some people advice and help them choose the right path in life.

I think this episode of depression was caused by a trigger in my life that made me hit rock bottom. My marriage broke down that was a big thing in my life. I always thought I would be successful at that. I don't give up easily. And then having another relationship that I invested a lot into and then when that failed, that really upset me. And my job situation changed, I went from one job to another. It's just a whole lot of things that can go wrong at a particular time. And then you can hit rock bottom.

I started feeling unsure of myself, and sad. Not all the time, but I have a lot of negative thoughts. I question my self worth. That's a really big thing for me. You think you are a failure where other people have setbacks. And then it just sort of gets worse and then emptiness is another feeling. You get empty and you don't have real joy in your life. It becomes difficult to find joy. I am quite good at hiding my unhappiness and pretending that everything is OK. Only you really know how you're feeling and sometimes you don't know what's going on. They're dark places.

I still think about self harm on a daily basis, but then I think of other things like my family, my kids, and I know it is not such a good idea.

I was lucky enough to have my brother, Anthony, who was aware my feelings weren't normal. It had gone on too long. I had no hesitation at all when he asked me 'mate do you ever think about hurting yourself?' and I said 'every day, every day'. I almost felt relieved. Anthony said we should go to the doctor and have a talk about it. It brought it to reality for me. As soon as Anthony said that, I said 'yeah make the appointment'. I don't think I would have made that step to go to the doctor. I probably would have just tried to handle it.

Anthony came with me to the doctor and told him what had been going on in the last six months. It was good to have that support, I couldn't have put what I was feeling into words. Anthony really looks after me, he has been my rock. Dad has been great too. We had a good chat about it, he actually asked me about it for the first time.

I feel like I am a stronger person now. I think accepting and understanding that I have depression was the first step. The realisation that what I felt is not normal—it is an illness. All those years where I felt ostracised or different all those sorts of things that I felt for such a long time, it was an illness.

Getting professional help is great because they teach you strategies. I learnt to recognise my feelings and whether or not it's an issue. My psychologist points me in the right direction. My true north. Even if I am thinking negatively she teaches me ways to deal with that thought. Don't push it down. She explains it like pushing down a ball under the water and that eventually you can't push it down anymore—it has to come back up. So rather than do that, just feel it—what shape it is, what colour it is, where it is, whether it is in your chest or in your tummy, close your eyes, what does it look like? Deal with it, recognise it and practice a bit of meditation, so breathe mindfully. I use to get panic attacks with the negative feelings. I don't have that anymore.

Exercise is really important to me. It's time to think about what I'm doing, being mindful. I think about my body running; what I'm seeing around me. The psychologists say to keep your mind on what you are actually doing in the moment rather than thinking about the negative thoughts.

To me, exercise is almost a punishment for my anguish. I should probably back it off a bit but it is a real outlet. I get a rush from it, I put myself through pain but I like the pain. Especially if I am having a really bad day or feeling angry. I can go out, do cardio exercise until I feel my heart about to explode. It is my self harm but it is positive. I am not taking to the bottle, I am just running, doing sprints and high cardio.

Exercise is important, laying off the booze is important. Alcohol is a depressant anyway. If I have been drinking a lot, I feel really flat the next day. Sleep is important—that is the good thing about the medication, it helps me sleep. Otherwise the negative thoughts come back.

It's an ongoing journey. I am a stronger person for it. I have my bad days still but I have a lot more good days than bad days. So I'm not sad all of the time now, just some of the time. I still get emotional talking about it.

I guess people don't really understand how it affects you. There is the word depression, people take that on but they don't really ask what that means. Depths of despair is how I would put it. Some people just think 'oh just snap out of it, you'll be right' but you just can't. I think depression can affect anyone, from any walk of life.

Mental illness awareness is becoming more prominent. When you go into the male toilets in a hotel or something like that there are those little picture frames with a message from Beyond Blue. Having those messages out there shows me I am not alone. Sometimes there are pictures of football players that have depression, with little messages of advice and that sort of stuff. I think that is good because people might look at that and go 'hey that's how I feel' or 'maybe I should go and get help'. Or just go and chat to someone. I always read the messages.

I am doing things now for the right reasons, to keep me happy and make sure they are the right decisions for me. I am just focusing on the kids and my family at the moment.

I am probably an emotional person. A lot of things can set me off, it can be something as silly as watching this TV show now and there might be a sad moment and I'm crying and my daughter Karah will look over at me a say 'are you OK Dad, are you alright?' It could just be a beautiful scene and I'll tear up. Stuff that you try to push down comes to the surface.

TIDY HOUSES

interview with
K R I S T E N   H A M M O N D
by Keira de Hoog

You can use vitamins to help a woman through those things.
~ TOM CRUISE (ON POSTNATAL DEPRESSION)

*I'm going to take a wild guess and say that Mr Cruise has
never suffered from postpartum depression.*
~ BROOKE SHIELDS (IN RESPONSE)

'You know what they say—a tidy house is a tidy mind. Pruning the roses was the outward manifestation of a voice that told me I had to be the perfect mother.'

❄   ❄   ❄

I'm sitting in a café on an autumnal Melbourne lunchtime with Kristen Hammond, mother of two, Maisy and Olive. Her daughters are 20 months apart, one starting high school, the other in her second-last year of primary school. One daughter has the same laid-back personality as Kristen's husband, Aaron, and the other is harder on herself, a lot like Kristen. A recent family photo of their road trip up the coast of Australia reflects a tight-knit, happy family unit. Proud parents, beautiful girls and a journey of great strength to get there.

'I didn't know I had postnatal depression at first,' says Kristen. 'That whole thing about your life just changing in an instant is true and I had no control. I remember getting my first nappy bag and thinking, I'm not a woman who carries a nappy bag around!'

She bites into a grain salad and shakes her head, laughing. 'I think that was the thing—having no control. So I developed these almost manic tendencies, just trying to keep abreast of everything.

'I distinctly remember having to prune the roses at home. I'd never gardened in my life—gardening ain't my thing! But the roses had to be pruned. I'd never cared about them before, and I've never cared about them since! They're right at the front of our house, on the porch. A good reflection of my mental state when my kids were young was if the roses were pruned or the porch was overflowing.'

We laugh at that, but the image stays with me for a long time afterwards—a set of porch stairs covered over in sharp thorns that block the entrance to her home. It's a reminder of how closed we keep ourselves in the times we really need help. How many other people have metaphoric gardens growing over their own mental health issues? Or perfectly pruned hedgerows making things seem so neat inside when they are actually chaotic?

Kristen is mindful that I am seven months pregnant with my first child. We discussed whether it was a good idea for me to conduct this interview with her on postnatal depression, but I am keen to hear the truth and what to expect if I go through any similar emotions myself. Education is vital at such a time in your life. That said, as my mum is fond of saying, 'ignorance is bliss', which I also believe up to a point—I'm happy to forgo stories on extreme labour pain where possible!

'With a new baby you spend a lot of time in your head,' Kristen explains. 'This is something that therapy helped a lot with later. But if I described my mental state with postnatal depression, my internal chatter would have been off the scale. I was talking to myself and being tough on myself all the time. The voice said to me, "Now you're a mum you have to have biscuits in the cupboard for when people drop around". 'Cause all of a sudden when you have a baby, people drop around! Or you'd always have to have different food in the house on offer, or you'd have to have all your washing done and the ironing, and that's what I thought a mother would do. I felt like if my housework wasn't done, then everyone was judging me.

'I think one of the things that medication and therapy really helps with is being able to turn that negative chatter right down, or turn it off, or allow me to be able to talk back to it rationally and to be able to say, "Don't be ridiculous" or not to let it speak of those sorts of things.

'I did a lot of nesting before the birth of my first baby, which I guess is a form of control as well. Crazy things like labelling my cupboards and telling my husband, "Aaron, my chocolates go here. Nowhere else". But it's all part of it. They say 85% of women experience mood changes with a baby, and so mine started … started … started, and then gradually got worse. I just didn't recognise it as depression. I think Aaron was probably wandering around the house on eggshells. I was thinking to myself, "Is this the new normal? Or is this a phase? Is this depression?"'

I stir my soup as it's too hot to eat yet, thinking about what Kristen is saying. I have to wonder what 'normal' will be like with our own new baby, and is there even such a thing? And therefore how hard it would be for someone who has depression on top of all the new skills and nappy changes and feeding rosters to separate the madness of new motherhood from an encompassing feeling of heaviness and uncertainty. Wouldn't you just think, 'This is life now' and so for a long time you don't get the necessary diagnosis or help?

Kristen continues, 'I'd had a miscarriage before I had Maisy, so when I found out I was pregnant again it was a really happy time. But it was kind of a trepidatious time too. Things like a miscarriage kind of knock you mentally. I think I spent quite a bit of time in the back of my head always a little bit fearful of losing this next baby. Which is not a great way to approach a pregnancy.

'When I finally gave birth to a healthy girl it became obvious that I'm a big planner and my list writing was out of control! I even remember in the hospital with Maisy, we hadn't even left yet and I had lists and lists and lists that were really, really long.' She shrugs helplessly. 'I'd get stressed out that I would forget something between thinking the thought and going to the list! I just wanted to be controlled and organised. I thought, "If I write it on the list I'll work it out". I wrote down every single feeding time, everything.'

I laugh. 'I am also a bit of a list maker,' I confess, 'although not the kind that springs up in bed and needs to write a thought down on a receipt with some lipstick. It can usually wait, or can be forgotten.' Together we wonder (and we're sure there's evidence to support this), whether people who have Kristen's kind of mindset are maybe more prone to depression. The strident list-makers. 'People who are always trying to control stuff. So you're harder on yourself when things go wrong,' Kristen says.

'Maisy was a terrible sleeper too, so that wouldn't have helped my darkening thoughts either,' she continues. 'She would wake up two or three times a night, which eventually did lessen. But then she would only ever nap for 45 minutes during the day. And 45 minutes is nothing. You've just sat down and had a drink or something, and maybe managed to look at the dishes and think about what might be for dinner before the baby's awake again. I couldn't function! We went to a sleep school. I think there's a lot to be said for getting that sorted! And I'm not saying you have to have a routine, but a baby that can sleep for good periods, and a mum that can go with the flow, rather than wanting complete order, is so much better.'

A waiter brings us glasses of water and I gulp mine down, constantly feeling dehydrated in the last months of pregnancy. I have a spoonful of soup and ask straight out, 'So when were you actually formally diagnosed with postnatal depression?'

'I saw a maternal child health nurse after the birth of Maisy. I'd go in there and talk to her and she'd look and me and go, "Hmm…". I know for my first few months of visits she was probably waiting for me to pull out of my mood. And then eventually she said, "I think I need to give you the test."'

Kristen explains that she answered a set of questions on a scale of one to five, and afterwards the nurse added up the responses to conclude whether she was suffering postnatal depression or not.

I looked this up online afterwards and discovered The Edinburgh Postnatal Depression Scale (EPDS), a set of screening questions that can indicate whether you have symptoms that are common in women with depression and anxiety during pregnancy and in the year following the birth of a child. For example, one of the questions is:

I have been able to laugh and see the funny side of things
☐ As much as I always could
☐ Not quite so much now
◉ Definitely not so much now
☐ Not at all

Kristen remembers the nurse did the test with her on the spot and told her then and there, 'OK, you've got postnatal depression. You need to go and see your doctor.'

'She had heard my stories about the roses, but most of all there's something about depression where I think I just had a flat affect. You can get yourself functioning but not enjoying anything. Although you're out there and you'd go to a shopping centre to have lunch with friends, or you'd see your mothers' group, I never felt engaged in anything. I was just there. The kind of feeling where I could be at a party with one hundred other people and I'd be miserable and feel so lonely. I couldn't connect with anyone.'

She shakes her head and her voice is strong and confident. She rests her salad fork in her bowl, picks up her water glass and declares, 'I feel like I spent years where I haven't been myself and now I feel like I'm myself—I can talk and I'm vibrant. I wasn't like that then. I was closed. So people who met me at that time didn't meet the real me.'

We clink over that. Lunchtime has picked up and people stream past our table ordering coffee and sandwiches. 'You mean the people in your mothers' group didn't know the real you?' I ask. 'Were they a good support for you at the time anyway?'

'In my mothers' group they spoke a little bit about postnatal depression but not much. It wasn't that they weren't supportive or didn't help, it's just I didn't know how to connect and tell people. After all, these were people I'd only recently met. There were a couple of other mums in my group who'd had "episodes" but nothing extended like me, at least that I know of. It's true that people don't talk about depression ... There was a woman who was in her forties and this was her only child, conceived through IVF. She got really bad mastitis six weeks after her son was born, and she tried to persist with breastfeeding but eventually, by about ten weeks, she was like, "Nuh, I can't do this anymore". So she kind of had a depressed period surrounding that and the whole anxiety of going through IVF which is very stressful in itself. But once she'd stopped breastfeeding and could feel like herself again and not ill, she bounced back.'

'Giving your depression a reason, like your health or a problem like mastitis, can be easier in a way don't you think?' I ask, thinking about being able to explain physical ailments versus explaining an unknown black cloud hanging over you.

'Yes,' agrees Kristen, 'I think I really struggled to actually feel like I had postnatal depression. Because I just felt for a long time that this is the new normal. This is what your life is now. Definitely things were changing right before Maisy was born, but the strength of my dark thoughts came on afterwards. Maisy was never in harm's way with me but there were definitely times when I would just have to leave the room and go "I can't deal with this". I'd go and ring Aaron. "Come home", I'd tell him, "I can't deal with this!"'

I wonder, 'Were you advised to take something for it then?'

'Yes, around that time I went to the doctor and she prescribed medication. I also went to see a psychologist and did sessions with her for a while.

'With a combination of these treatments, leading up to my second daughter Olive's birth, I kind of got to a good point. But I was worried it might happen again. The difference this time was though, that I was medicated with anti-depressants all the way through the second pregnancy and shortly after. Everything was looking good, although I remember my mother-in-law and my father complaining about our choice of Olive's name! Aaron got angry with them and told them, "This woman's depressed and you're making her life difficult!" So we kept her name as it was!

'After I had Olive, I went to the doctor and said, "OK I'm good, I don't want to take anti-depressants anymore". So I weaned off them. But around this time, while I was still pregnant with Olive, Aaron started his own business. That was really challenging. A couple of years after having both girls, I was doing lots of stuff for him and the new business, and wasn't on medication. And the financial stress of it—the stress of having your own business tipped me back over the edge.'

Someone bumps into the side of our table with a handbag and gives me a fright. I unconsciously grab my stomach as if to protect it and Kristen holds onto her rattling drink. I wave at them unconsciously, forgiving.

'I remember going back to the doctor and saying, "OK, I'll go back on the medication"' Kristen continues. 'I saw another counsellor at that point—a family counsellor who wasn't a psychologist as such. I love therapy and recommend it to everyone. A couple of hours talking about yourself with someone totally non-judgemental, someone who doesn't know your family history or the ins and outs of your life is great. Someone who can go, "But don't you think this is what they might think?" and just provide a rational and sane voice.

'I was also seeing the counsellor weekly because my doctor was concerned I was going to kill myself.'

She adds this point nonchalantly at the end, and I wonder if I've misheard. 'Really?' I ask her. She nods. I've worked with Kristen for a couple of years and just can't see her like that—she is an incredibly well-organised person and a very capable, busy and amazing mother.

'It's true,' she says. 'That was my worst period with depression—worse than after Maisy was born. I think my brain or neural pathways know how to get to the point of depression now. So without medication, it is easier for my brain to take that well-trodden path to depression ever so quickly. I feel it can go even beyond where I have been before.'

We liken it to a muscle stretching over time and getting more and more flexible. It makes sense that your mind can do this too, but in a detrimental direction. 'I look back on it now and I think it's amazing Aaron and I are still together,' admits Kristen. 'He never walked away but he didn't know what to do either. I remember one night having a screaming fight with him at one end of the hallway and me at the other end. We were just fighting about the business and money but it was part of a bigger picture of "I can't cope here". I do remember in that conversation when I went, "I just want to die. Nobody's going to care if I'm not here. My being here is not helping. And if I die there's insurance money and everybody will be so much better off."

'One day I just left the house and drove to Healesville, and sat in the pub there all day. It kind of felt like if I wasn't there, all my problems would go away. But they don't, they go with you. And eventually you've gotta go back and face it. So that kind of temporary leaving … I think I just got to the point where I was thinking I'm just going to leave the world altogether. 'Cause that ends it.

'I never got a razor blade or anything like that. More thoughts where you're sitting in the car thinking, "I could just veer off the road and drive into a tree". I often had dark thoughts at that time about jumping out of a plane. Or I'm on a bus and I'm just going to open the door while it's still going. I don't know what pulls you back from this and compels you not to. I think I probably needed that one more thing to push me over the edge. Whatever the one more thing was …'

I shake my head, amazed at her ability to phrase these thoughts and feelings from such a dark time. I wonder, 'Just how hard is it for partners to deal with someone suffering postnatal depression, or depression in general, when they talk about killing themselves?'

'I think for Aaron, and for any partner, you must feel so utterly helpless. What do I do for this person? I don't know what to do. Partners are the ones who love you and stick with you. They're the kind of person who can't get peeved at you. Your friends can, but they can't. They just have to keep working with you on it. They live with it every day and really see the ugly side of it, because a lot of people keep it all so hidden.'

'And your girls?' I ask her. 'Did they know about these feelings?'

'My girls were too young at the time. But I certainly remember having moments where I'd be on the bed just crying and they'd say "Oh, Mummy's sad". And my not being able to stop just because they were there. Knowing I can't pull myself together just because you're seeing me sad. It's not going to work like that.'

I ruminate that this is maybe where medication is important not just for the person suffering from depression, but also for their carers, their loved ones and their families, to help them and to create a normal life instead of what could be a terrible and fractured one. Kristen agrees. 'Whenever I took medication, I was always anticipating when I would stop taking it. I'd always thought, "That's good, it will get me to where I'm better and then we'll phase it off". But I remember having a conversation with my doctor where she told me, "It's like you're a diabetic and you have to take medication every day. And if you're a person whose brain knows how to get to this point, for you to be able to function every day in a stable ongoing manner, this is what you need to do."

'I really resisted that, 'cause I really didn't want to take medication—"Why can't I be healthy and normal?" I don't know if it was the stigma, although maybe it was in some ways. But then I got to a point where I was taking the medication and feeling so good. Why would I give that up? Why would I go back to screaming at Aaron? Why would I go back to screaming in the hallway and telling him I want to kill myself? What a horrible thing to do to another person. I wasn't doing it deliberately or maliciously, it was just how I felt. How could I put my family through that again?

'Aaron was worse than me in the no-medication stakes, coming from the perspective that you don't need it. But I think his recent diagnosis with diabetes has been a bit of a wake up for him—he can't function every day without medication either!'

I nod, glad that her partner and others are hopefully understanding more and more the need for medication for mental health and it not just being some form of 'cop out' but a necessity. The waiter comes to collect our empty dishes, and amidst the crockery clatter we realise the café is still buzzing with life. Kristen rests forward on her elbows on the cleared space, gazing around us.

'I just know that I wouldn't give this feeling up for the world,' she says. 'And I can't have this feeling without medication, or if I can, it's only temporary. I certainly put on weight with the medication but it got to a point where it's either that or feeling terrible. I'm just on a set dosage and go and see my doctor every six months for a new script and just continue taking it.'

She brushes a few stray grains off her elbows and continues, 'I couldn't say that my experience or enjoyment of motherhood would have been any different if I hadn't been depressed. I mean, it's just such a huge change in your life.' She smiles at me, apologetic, my naivety reflected back in an unknowing grin.

'Maybe I would have felt all those things anyway, and maybe I got as much enjoyment out of being a mum at that time as I would have ever got out of it. The difference was my not being able to react to things in a normal emotional way. But none of this has affected my relationship with my daughters. I think if my depression continued unabated or I continued to insist on weaning off medication, then they're obviously now of an age to understand what depression is. But even earlier, maybe from seven or eight, they would have been at age where they could go, "Mummy's not right". I would have hated that. I would have hated it if they ever felt like that.'

I ask her about sharing her story with other people. 'Did you ever have people who didn't understand, or treated you differently or worse because of your experience?'

'No,' says Kristen. 'I didn't really experience any great stigma. But I do wonder, again, in the theme of accepting physical ailments over mental illness, whether postnatal depression is easier to accept and draws less of a stigma because there's an event that precedes it. You do undergo a hormonal change that people can understand. But in the eye of the storm it was very difficult to articulate what I was experiencing. I don't think I didn't talk about depression for fear of experiencing stigma, it was just that I didn't know how to. Now I feel trepidatious about forthcoming hormonal changes in my life. Like menopause, I'm thinking, "Really?! Do I have to go and do all of this again?" That's probably another reason not to give up my medication.

'You can't live your life worrying though, which is hard for someone who is a big pre-planner. I wouldn't wish it on my worst enemy, but in hindsight I'm not sure if I would change any of it. It has given me a much richer appreciation of being well and really valuing my mental health.'

'That's great,' I say. 'Does it take a lot to manage your mood, even now?'

'I am always aware of trying to do stuff to keep it in check. I try to meditate; I've never been a journal writer, but that kind of thing. And I'm more conscious now of stopping to smell the roses. No more pruning! The journey was worth it for the person I am now. But it might have been different if I'd lost Aaron or harmed the girls, even just mentally. Exercise really helps. There's probably quite a strong correlation between my mental health and when I am exercising and when I am not. I reckon if I sat down and was able to keep a journal, you'd probably find that at the times I was really bad I wasn't exercising.' I nod at this. I know from my own experience that mood and fitness are very closely linked. The endorphins after a workout or even a quick walk outdoors are sometimes enough to lift you out of life's fog whenever you descend into one. A great friend of mine had experienced bouts of depression off and on since adolescence and only recently took up yoga, which has helped him considerably. 'Loosened body, loosened mind', he says.

'From your experience,' I ask Kristen, 'how would you help others going through postnatal depression?'

She thinks for a bit—it's a tough question. 'If my sister or a good friend had postnatal depression it would depend on them how I would help,' she says. 'Because I wouldn't have wanted help, especially with housework and practical things. That would have stressed me out more. I do worry about family or friends who go through IVF, as they're likely to have hormones going crazy. And if they have been depressed before, I can see that they could easily get there.

'It's a really hard one. Interestingly though, a good friend of mine's sister had been having rounds of IVF and has just had her first child. My friend had gone over to her sister's house one day, seen her and told her, "You're not well, you're seriously depressed. I'm taking you to the hospital right now". I didn't see her sister at that time. But I don't know if I'd ever "see" depression in a person, even someone I loved. What would I expect to see, that would make me call someone to look after their child and then take them to a hospital for treatment? I don't know that you necessarily say things that would alarm others and make them "see" depression, such as you want to harm yourself or your baby. It depends on the person and how open they are with you I guess. I was never open with anyone at the time, except Aaron.

'As it turns out, my friend was right and her sister was admitted to a psychiatric hospital. She had postnatal psychosis, the next step on from postnatal depression. So she was in hospital for quite a long time, maybe six or eight weeks without her baby. I also had another who was hospitalised and subsequently diagnosed with bipolar disorder. There was no indication of it before she had children.

'I think you just have to be there for that person. You have to be an ear. I would definitely be encouraging anybody who I thought was even close to being depressed to be seeing their doctor. My doctor was fantastic. I'd never seen a psychologist before having kids. But I loved it. It's hard work though, talking, crying to somebody for an hour about yourself. I can see the value in talking to somebody about it. I couldn't have said to people I knew the things that I said to her.

'One of my close friends has depression and in my dealings with her it's always been, "Come on, let's go out for a walk" or "Let's go and do some shopping". Because I know when I went through it, all I wanted to do was spend all my time in bed. I just wanted to close the curtains and shut the world out and lie down all the time. By virtue of having a baby though you can't just stay in bed. They want to be fed, or they need attention and this makes you keep going. I wonder what there is for people without a baby to lure them out of it. What can draw them back into the world? Often it is only them and their choice to return—it just takes time and patience from others. I remember a gorgeous cartoon of someone who was depressed, and a friend coming up to them and asking if they could just sit with them. The friend builds a comforting looking nest out of blankets, and together they sit side by side. Nothing more is needed or expected.'

'And now?' I ask Kristen. 'You are 100%?'

'My internal voice is still there but it's not what it was'. She smiles. 'I think women are naturally harder on themselves, so the internal voice is hideous to start with. I don't know if kids have an internal chatter—I don't remember having one when I was a kid. But I reckon Maisy's would be so nice to her and so forgiving. Whereas I think Olive is a bit more hard on herself. But one of the things that I do—and I think schools do this really well now—are resilience projects with external speakers who come in and talk to them about being resilient and being happy and being accepting. So they're taught a lot more about those sorts of mental health things that really help. And I've talked to the girls about being nice to themselves. I think my thing now is to set them up with the kind of skills that will help them cope and to not get to where I got to.

'But being well, I can now listen to my inner voice and move it aside. Whereas previously I wasn't able to step outside it, so it was the only voice I had. Now I can have a conversation with it.'

I ask about the roses on the porch these days and she laughs.

'Pruning the roses was the outward manifestation of a voice that told me I had to be perfect. And I tied myself up in knots doing it. The roses are still there and they're unpruned!'

We stand up and walk out of the café. I still have my old dictaphone in one hand, recording the conversation. I'm glad I do because as we head back to work, still talking about recovery, I ask, 'How would you like to finish your story?' and Kristen says:

'This is for my daughters but also for Aaron. I am finally able to step outside and look back at my period of depression from the viewpoint of someone who feels well again. Not to apologise for it, but just to be grateful. I can't believe you've stuck with me; I'm so lucky to have you. You always stepped up and tried to do whatever you felt was going to help me. Often those things were the wrong thing, but just the fact that someone keeps trying means everything.'

For more information or if you or a loved one are experiencing feelings of post natal depression, PANDA is the National Perinatal Depression Helpline, funded by the Australian and Victorian Governments. It provides vital support, information, referral and counselling to thousands of Australian parents and their families. Callers do not need to have a diagnosis of antenatal or postnatal depression to make contact with the Helpline. Visit www.panda.org.au

BIRTHMARKS

J A I N E   E I R A

My mother was just sixteen when she met my father. He was twenty-three.

She had three kids by the time they divorced.

At twenty-nine, she aimed her car at a pole, doing ninety.

Now she has an invisible scar running from the top of her ear, down to her knee. I say invisible, because only she ever sees it, and yet she hates that one more than all the others. The 'F' on her wrist, I think she's even fond of. But aren't they all just self-inflicted?

I was six when she decided to send us away. All our stuff packed up in milk crates in the hall, a gift atop each. My sister was four when she told my uncle—upon receipt of a big stuffed panda bear—that presents do not make it better.

I was ten when my hair started falling out, from stress, and fourteen when I ran away. I look at my mother now—now that we have found each other again—and we are so similar. The signs are all there. I look down at my own scars: at the cigarette burns given me by a boy on the streets, and the silver slash-marks I added later.

How can you call them self-inflicted? They seem more like birthmarks than anything else.

'F' is for fuck, she tells me.

moosekleenex.tumblr.com

AN ANECDOTE REGARDING MY BLEACH-BASED BOYHOOD AND WHAT MIGHT HAVE CAUSED IT

D A N   C H R I S T I E

As a boy of eight I was possessed by the malignant spirit of a late 19th century parlour maid.

I had no interest in misbehaviour or mucking around in the dirt or Auskick practice on the weekends. No, no. My notion of joy was to be arm-deep in suds at the sink after my parents' dinner parties, or vacuuming the hallway to Buckingham Palace standard.

Excited by the thought of possessing my own range of cleaning implements, I'd look for creative ways of transforming inanimate objects into anything that could be used in my artillery of domestic weapons. An old, neglected t-shirt was reinvented in my youthful hands as a first-rate polishing cloth. A broken shuttlecock, cleverly bound to a stick by a few good metres of masking tape, proved a most effective cobwebber. And a woollen pom pom was appropriated for my personal use as a natty duster.

And, like a late 19th century parlour maid, I sat in my pantry—when off duty of course—in deep contemplation of the more important questions regarding domestic efficiency. Should I use a little less beeswax on the sideboard to make it go further? How much silver polish is too much silver polish?

It was a passion that became an obsession. As my fellow peers fiddled with playground games and Jurassic Park trading cards, I'd be thinking of new ways to wash the windows and order the cutlery, and tutt-tutting as I considered the chaotic state of my young brother's disgraceful pigsty of a bedroom!

It was a unique and nervous life I lead back then. I was so uncertain of how I belonged. I now know that this obsession with cleaning was related to my struggle to socialise with kids my own age. You see, at age eight, and all my time growing up, I flat out assumed that most people didn't like me. I was weird, a sissy, a premature adult and not a proper boy at all. Of course, I now understand that these perceptions were misguided and influenced largely by the fact that, even now, I suffer from social anxiety. But as a child, unsure how to relate to other boys, cleaning gave me something to do and filled me with sense of purpose. It was a practical and productive way to cope, a worthwhile use of the time that I couldn't bear to spend with other people.

Other kids were normal; I knew that I wasn't. Everyone else behaved one way, I thought and behaved another. I was terrible at sport, liked staying indoors and preferred watching costume dramas on television to watching cartoons. As much as a part of me wanted to, I knew I could never play the role of the average suburban kid. So to deal with these emotions, I cleaned. I thought it gave me positive reinforcement. My mum praised me for it and that praise made me feel better about myself. Yet, in truth, I would have given anything to stop the cleaning, to stop worrying, to feel relaxed and happy instead. It was a frustrating and isolating life, everything felt scary and out of sync. Time and time again I would think: What on earth am I doing in here, in Mooroolbark, Australia in 1993? It was as if I had been transported from another time, and other place, and thrown into a century that I couldn't possibly belong in.

In fact, at the time, I considered my place in the world so ridiculous, that eventually I came to believe there had been some sort of strange cosmic mix-up. Another force, quite beyond my control, was clearly at work as I haunted the rooms of my childhood home brandishing my sad and ragged duster. My theory was this: I became convinced that, by a slip of physics, and through some bizarre mix-up in the space-time continuum, as I manically removed the dust from my present-day family home, simultaneously, in some manor house, in late 19th century England, I had utterly and completely switched places with some poor and unsuspecting parlour maid.

I could see it in my head. There she was, going about her daily routine, diligently scrubbing at knobs and straightening pictures. Then, for no apparent reason, seeing the master of the household walking ahead of her down the passage, the parlour maid felt a strange and sudden urge to drop her rag, fix her gaze, and run full-bolt up the corridor, taking what to modern eyes would look like an absolutely massive specky of AFL Grand Final proportions! Or perhaps that wasn't how it happened. Possibly, instead of serving the guests at dinner, the tragic maid was caught out, by the outraged head butler, giggling loudly with the master's children in the house larder. What would have appeared to the 19th century onlooker as an act of supreme insubordination and disrespect, to us, would have looked like nothing more than a grown woman, in a white frilly cap, deeply engrossed in a child's game of eating disgusting foods incorporating soot, half a pound of bacon and the lord's oldest and very best champagne.

I wonder if, had this little glitch not occurred and this confusion been put right, I would have put down my dishcloth and gone outside to play? Would I have learned to have more fun, not to worry so much and to feel more relaxed around other kiddies my age? As I reflect on my childhood, I do wonder, if this space-time mix-up had been reversed, and everything had gone according to the set and standard order of things, would the poor maid have kept her job, and would my parents' good wedding china, that priceless discontinued range of crockery imported especially from Germany, have survived the 1990s without the chips and cracks created by well-intentioned but very slippery eight-year-old hands?

Maybe that would have been the case. But then, if I sacrificed a little too much of my youth to the scrubbing brush, I also like to think that my 19th century double got something rather satisfying out of her end of the deal. I hope, after years of scraping and toiling and a lifetime of answering yes-sir-no-sir-of-course-what-ever-you-wish-sir, that, for a few days at least, she finally and gloriously had the chance to let herself go. No more tasteful discretion and humble gratitude. No. Instead, I see her high on the spirit of an eight-year-old boy, breaking, kicking and cackling her way through those stuffy and privileged halls.

Not stopping to think about her actions and listening to absolutely no one, I imagine her tearing at every tradition ever imposed upon her. I see her sliding down the bannisters and yelling at the top of her voice. There she is, diving into the ornamental fountain and dashing across the antiquated rooftops. Look at her, exploring long-forgotten attics and sprinting though the manicured hedges with a mischievous sense of adventure. The lord has no concept of how to deal with this. Instead, he just looks on in confusion as, one by one, the maid breaks every petty little rule she was so used to obeying. She's throwing off each shackle of her repressive existence, laughing, singing and having the absolute time of her life. She is joyous, fabulous, a rebellious source of absolute chaos, unburdened, fearless and finally free on what was, once upon a time, a most quiet and ordered estate.

Adapted from the original, published in *Death of A Scenester* magazine, 2012.

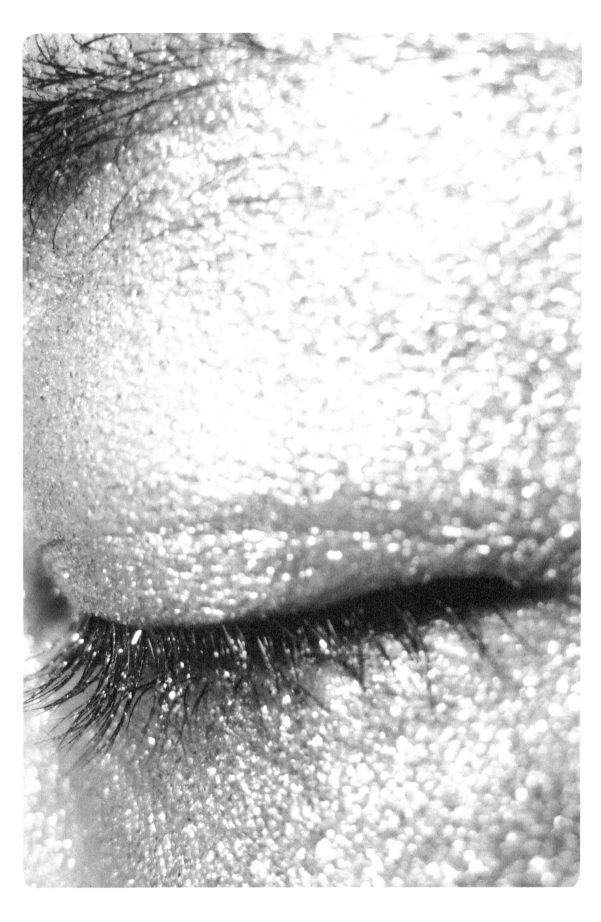

TRICHOTILLOMANIA AND ME

CARMEL PARDY

When I was pulling my eyelashes out it was like I went into this bubble. I was unreachable when I was pulling.

I can't remember exactly when I started pulling my eyelashes out but I know that when I first began to do it (around primary school age) it was just something I discovered I could do. I liked the feel of it and I liked the way I could make my eyelid click as I did it. I was so excited about my discovery I showed my brother what I could do and even tried to pull his eyelashes out. I can still remember the moment, the two of us standing together in the bathroom trying to do it to one another. When I reflect on this I do believe that this was just innocent childhood exploration. But then I crossed the line. I can't remember when or how but at some point I realised that pulling my eyelashes had become something more sinister. I knew that it was no longer something I should share with anyone and indeed something that I now had to lie about when asked 'What happened to your eyes?' (Anyone with trichotillomania will know the excruciating feeling when someone confronts you about your darkest secret.)

People with trichotillomania will tell you that for a long time they thought they were the only person in the world with such an affliction. I believed there was something really wrong with me and that I was just no good.

Trichotillomania is the compulsion to pull out one's hair, but it is just as important to acknowledge the secrecy of the condition. People with tricho are vigilant about maintaining their secret. I believe this component of the condition is important to treat—possibly more important than just focusing on the act of pulling.

Often people with tricho will feel embarrassed that it is such a bizarre behaviour, but I've seen people without tricho pull the odd hair out and have watched them complete the same ritual that a person with tricho would. This tells me that the act of pulling is not so weird—it's normal in a way. But when you cross the line, and pull your hair so much that you cause damage and it impacts on your whole life, it really is a serious matter. And it's the intensity of the pulling and the absolute intensity of the urges and the secrecy surrounding this condition that make it bizarre.

Pulling out my eyelashes impacted on my whole life. It shaped the person I was and how I presented to the world. I was affected by it when I was pulling, and it was present even in the moments I wasn't pulling. That is, I got through the day with the knowledge that I would have relief by night, pulling my eyelashes out.

When I decided to share my personal story, I asked myself what I really wanted people to know and understand about trichotillomania. I kind of thought that someone without tricho might read about it and then say, 'oh that's that thing where you just pull your hair out' as if it's something a person does casually without thinking. So I want to try and really capture what it is like for someone with trichotillomania. I want to describe to you, if I can, what life with tricho was really like for me.

Pulling my eyelashes out was the way I started the day and the way I ended the day for many years, probably 30 years. When I was a child I can remember being curled up in bed hiding under the blankets just pulling my eyelashes out in chunks. Then I became more refined with my pulling, pulling one eyelash out at a time. By the time I was 15 I had no eyelashes and by the time I was in year twelve I had no eyelashes and ridiculous half eyebrows. I mainly pulled at night-time. The damage was obvious but I was very alone with this situation. I received no help, in fact no one in my family discussed it. No one told me to stop doing it and no one reached out to me either. I left home at 18 and my pulling advanced, pulling whenever I had the opportunity, morning, during the day and night. I could spend hours in a 24-hour period pulling. Sometimes I couldn't get out of bed because I had to keep pulling or I couldn't go to sleep at night because I had to pull. If I fell asleep and woke up in the middle of the night I would pull then too. It was very exhausting and I feel very sad about how consumed I have been by this condition. Sometimes it would take me days to get one particular eyelash. It would be so small but I could feel it, and I'd want it out. The intensity of this kind of urge was crippling. I could spend many sessions on one eyelash. I would have to contort my head in a peculiar way or pull my eyelid so tightly and press my fingers together so hard to get it out. Sometimes in these moments the intensity was so great that I feared my eye might fall out or I would have a heart attack. At times like this, I fantasised about being locked away and being restrained to a bed, so that I could no longer do it. One time I even got up out of bed and drove to an all night chemist to buy some tweezers to help me in my mission. I snuck out of the house while my partner slept, bought the tweezers, went home, pulled the eyelash out and hopped back into bed. And I would carry on the next day as if life was normal.

In one of these intense sessions of pulling I did so much damage that my eye swelled up and bled. I could not go to work, so I lay in bed depressed and lonely and listened to the ABC. It just so happened to be OCD and anxiety week in about 1994 and they were talking about OCD and happened to mention trichotillomania. I couldn't believe it. That was my first moment of realising there must be others. It was not long after that that I read a chapter on tricho in a book about OCD. From that day I just stopped pulling. I probably went a hundred days without pulling. I thought I was cured!! This was an exciting time for me and I met others with tricho at a support group and I even shared my story the following year at a conference.

I guess I would say that this was the beginning of my recovery, but my journey since then has been a long one. For the next 16 years I continued my battle with trichotillomania. That first 100 days was the longest period I had of not pulling, until recently. In that period between then and now I muddled along. I have been in and out of therapy for years. I made the decision not to ever use medication because I really understood that the act of pulling out my eyelashes was something I did to myself, it wasn't something that just happened to me. It was a direct affront on myself, that I did. I went through Cognitive Behavioural Therapy (CBT) with psychiatrists and psychologists at different times. The most useful thing I got from this was learning how much I loathed myself. I had no self-esteem, and little confidence or belief in myself, despite the fact that I was very competent in many areas of my life. Yet my inner self was in turmoil and had been for a very long time. I also realised from doing CBT that I was in a constant state of ambivalence and making the smallest decision caused me angst. I was competent in a crisis but experienced everyday sort of anxiety all the time. On the outside I appeared to be functioning but my inner world was horrible. Having tricho is like living a double life.

For much of this time I guess I just quietly battled on. I focused on general self-awareness and tried to develop an understanding of my relationship with my trichotillomania. My tricho has been both friend and foe. I've been very defeated by it at many times and then had times of acceptance, which has also been useful. In these times of trying to accept it, I'd not focus on stopping the pulling and would just think this is a part of me and acknowledge that it's had a purpose in my life. It got me through a volatile childhood, university degrees, being in unsavoury relationships, becoming a mother, and it provided me with the only way I knew of getting some peace.

It sounds strange, but I guess that's what I haven't gone into yet, how can such a destructive behaviour provide one with peace? When I was pulling my eyelashes out it was like I went into this bubble. I was unreachable when I was pulling. I had a need to create this bubble around me. I think it was kind of like, if I hurt myself no one else could or if others inflicted pain on me it would not penetrate and it stopped me from being completely present. So it was like a shield, my protector.

It affected the way I related to people—I couldn't be completely present and completely intimate even with those I loved most. For much of my life, my trichotillomania has kept me in a very solo place in the world. Not even those I love most could penetrate that bubble, because I have been vigilant with maintaining the secrecy and intricacies of my trichotillomania.

I have lived with the fear of being discovered by my partner and my children, and have I dreaded having to explain it to them. My children were getting to the point when on a couple of occasions they noticed my eyes and pointed out to me that I hardly had any eyelashes. I can't explain how devastating and frightening that was for me, that my little girls would be exposed to this demon in my life. I could no longer be relaxed with my children and sadly I could not have those intimate moments of lying with them, just looking into their eyes. I kind of pushed them away for fear of being found out and because I wanted to protect them. I knew I had to do something.

Another jolting moment I had was when I was alone in my bedroom pulling out my eyelashes and one of my babies was crying, really crying. I could not go to her. I did not know whether she was hurt or whether she was safe, but I just had to keep pulling. I was in that bubble and not even my baby's cry could penetrate it. This frightened me and I realised how much trichotillomania controlled me. My world of tricho was impacting on others, and this saddened me.

I think it was the accumulation of all that I have told you that led me to finally say 'no more'. I was tired—pulling out my eyelashes had consumed so much of me for so many years. I then had this moment where I knew my life had to change. I could not go on like this anymore. At this point of my journey I sometimes had pull-free days, sometimes weeks, yet even this was not enough. I had this conviction that I wanted it to stop completely, I no longer wanted to manage it, I wanted to live my life more fully and I wanted to live my life true to myself. I made the commitment to myself then, that my life would change. I didn't know how, but I knew that that was what needed to happen. To do this, I knew I needed to believe in myself.

So, I decided to run a marathon. I had to unravel the mystery of the marathon. Running has been very useful to me in my journey. It's simply one foot in front of the other. Breathing in and breathing out. The pain and suffering of running is to me like the pain and suffering of life—you just experience it and you get through it. Running has enabled me to be in my mind and body, connecting the two. And it has taught me to be very in the moment and present, something that tricho has not enabled me to do. I cried a lot through my training, visualising myself crossing the finish line. I had a mantra I often said and that was, 'when you cross the line calm, your life will change forever'. I remained committed to this. I crossed the finish line and knew, once and for all, that I could believe in myself. People said to me 'How do you run 42km?' and I quietly knew that endurance wasn't a problem for me—I mean pulling your eyelashes out for 30 years? That's what I call endurance.

I didn't stop pulling straight away but I remained committed to my mission. I had made an appointment with a new therapist prior to the marathon and started therapy shortly after. As a result of having tricho, I have found it hard to have authentic relationships, and I knew that I had to learn to trust the person I was going to see and in some ways develop an attachment to her, one that provided me with the security to really delve into the depths that I have not wanted to go. I believe that this relationship has been crucial to my healing. I knew that this time, if I was really going to rid my life of trichotillomania, I really had to talk about 'it', and I knew I had to entrust my vulnerability in another human, the therapist—something I was not accustomed to doing. I had to face my trichotillomania head on. It was no longer useful to count how many days I stopped pulling or to try and will myself to stop pulling. I didn't even think about doing this. Really, what I have done is to try and unravel the secrecy of the tricho and have explored what is beneath that, sharing the real me with another human.

When I made the commitment to rid my life of tricho, I knew that I wanted to start living a life that is true to me. So what I unravelled was a lot of pain and sadness that I have not been able to face, and that my tricho had actually kept me at a distance from. This has been incredibly painful—to sit with one's sadness and to sit with life's disappointments—but it was what I have needed to do and what I had been avoiding for so long. My therapist enabled me to go into the bubble that I go into when I pull, but of course without pulling—this was a cathartic experience.

I am now in my ninth month of not pulling. I have no urges at all which is just extraordinary, as any person with tricho would know, and I believe the capacity to sit with my pain has enabled me to stop. It has almost been an organic process. I haven't had to resist urges as such, I just stopped. But it has taken a long time to get to this. I sometimes have the sensation of my eyelashes being pulled out. This probably happens daily and is sometimes horrible and makes me feel sick, but I guess this is some sort of trauma or result that I may have to live with as a result of inflicting so much trauma upon myself. This part of my journey—and I'm only in the early stages of it—has been so hard emotionally and there have been times when I thought it was much easier when I pulled. I guess I had this fantasy that when I stopped my life would be bliss—and, just quietly, it is pretty great, but I'm not shouting with excitement. I think I'm recovering from the exhaustion of living my life with such a debilitating, all-consuming condition.

Although I feel tired, I do feel a sense of relief. I'm scared sometimes, because I'm aware that I could start pulling again and that would devastate me, to return to that life frightens me. But for now I'm free. I can wake up in the morning and lie peacefully, comfortable in my own skin, I can look my girls in the eyes and love them as they deserve to be loved without feeling like I'm going to be found out and that I'm not good enough for them. I have moments now where I realise I'm just being, I'm in the moment and I'm alright. I no longer have to hide and I can have an honest and intimate relationship with my partner, my soulmate. And I can just be in the world now, content with being ME.

Thank you for reading my story. I hope that it may give other sufferers the courage to continue their difficult journey towards recovery, I hope that it may give family and friends of sufferers insight into the pain that your loved one feels and I hope that it may encourage professionals to look beyond the behaviour and to really see the person you are working with. Thank you for this opportunity.

OCD

I saw my future travelling alongside others and helping, and at the same time being inspired. For me I have learnt a lot of things about myself. I have more self-belief and I know there is hope.

HI MY NAME IS WENDY

I hope that what I share with you will give you a glimpse into the real life impact of anxiety disorders on sufferers and their families, and a greater understanding and insight into the severity and complexity of anxiety disorders, depression and OCD. I would like to start by talking about my experiences with anxiety and depression and in particular to talk to you about my journey with OCD. From the age of nine I had an enormous pre-occupation with religious views, fearing and feeling that I had sinned and must go to confession. I was tormented by fears, thoughts and memories. I would remember all those 'bad things' that I thought I had done and needed to go to confession for forgiveness several times a week. It was terrifying. I was scrupulous about the rules of the church and would be horrified about intrusive thoughts that would come into my head, all my thoughts and actions felt like sins. The pain, anguish, fear of God, the fear of hell did not allow my mind any time for rest. Among other reasons, I feel my OCD behaviours developed in response to anxious and stressful life events. I felt out of control, having thoughts and feelings that totally consumed me, and I had difficulty thinking of anything else. It was distressing, exhausting and time-consuming. When battling OCD, one is never at peace for any length of time. If peace steals into the heart unobserved, the scrupulous OCD sufferer feels guilty over feeling peaceful. I had other co-morbid conditions, these included anorexia, social anxiety and depression. I moved to Wodonga 16 years ago having lived in Melbourne all my life. The move to Wodonga changed my life! A local psychiatrist immediately diagnosed my condition as OCD. I had been misdiagnosed for over 30 years. This was the first step on my road to recovery. Having previously been treated for anorexia I had never heard of OCD until then, but I now know that many people suffer with OCD, in fact about 600,000 people in Australia, and still climbing. Many of these people suffer in silence because people with OCD are very aware that their obsessive thoughts and compulsive behaviours are excessive and irrational. When you know this, but feel you can't do anything about it, it makes you feel ashamed and embarrassed. So you don't tell anyone and find ways to hide it. It is often called the hidden disorder.

LIVING WITH OCD

OCD takes many different paths and I have suffered from many of them. From the debilitating, tormenting, obsessional thoughts, a super sense of responsibility towards others, cleanliness, fear of cancer, contamination fears, absolute super detail, to the rituals of checking, washing, cleaning, hoarding and mental compulsions too. The amount of time I spent thinking, worrying and ruminating was unbelievable. I even had fear of thinking about things, worrying that I would think thoughts before I had even thought them. (Thinking that you are going to think something bad, wrong, defective, whatever it may be.) I see this as ridiculous now, but at the time it was very, very real. I had an obsessive fear of knives and sharp objects for fear of hurting my children or others. I'd shake and shake my head to get rid of these thoughts and at the same time try to interrupt the thoughts by making a noise or noises say 'no, no, no', but they just wouldn't go! Eventually I'd have to shout 'no, no, no', until I was so distressed I would collapse in a heap. The harder I tried to get rid of the thoughts the more they stayed. I know better now. I was terrified of hurting others. If I drove over a bump in the road I would believe I had run over someone. I had to drive back and check the road, then drive back again, and again several times. Logic told me 'Wendy you couldn't have run anyone over' but you know, the illogical mind always won. Then having to look in the next day's newspaper to check for fatal accidents in that area. Thoughts and actions were illogical and irrational, but I was trapped by their powerful control, like being stuck in a spider's web. The harder I tried to climb out, the further I was pulled in. Another OCD symptom that affected my life—mind you, there were many, many more!—was imagining I hadn't washed my hands and I'd infect others or contaminate foodstuffs! Then something bad would happen! An illness or death would happen because of my thoughts or actions!!

Then there was:

SHOPPING

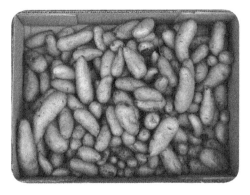

for potatoes—I'd stare and stare at each potato imagining harmful green patches. What will I do, if I make people sick? They might die!! Tomatoes, carrots, everything stared at, scrutinised and checked! No slashed butter packages. No bumps or dints on my packets or tinned products. Trying to wait for people to leave the aisles then painfully realigning tins on the supermarket shelves in case they fell on someone and it was my fault.

PERFECT BANANAS

were a necessity, with a lot of staring, feeling, touching, weighing and rejecting. Sometimes I'd have to leave. It was too traumatic. Whenever I did buy some, I would take them home, hide them, place them in a line of 'bestness', the perfect banana would be mine. You know what, by the time I ate them, they had brown spots or patches on them anyway. Grapes too, the biggest, best, golden coloured grapes.

HOARDING

lots and lots of stuff, especially food. In the freezer tiny pieces of food pedantically wrapped up in endless pieces of cling wrap, for future eating. Once I had 18 boxes of cornflakes, which were soft before they could be eaten. When I moved house I had enough toilet rolls and cleaning products for a year. I had a fear of running out of anything, even time.

FEAR OF AUTHORITY FIGURES

God, priests, doctors, police, even the bloomin' red light cameras. There was so much relief when we moved to Wodonga—no red light cameras!

Checking the car over and over—doors locked, handbrake on and off until it felt right, lights flicking on and off till I was sure they were off, checking over and over, then feeling if the windows were closed tight. Afraid to drive 1kph over the speed limit. Paranoid of speed cameras here in the streets of Wodonga, driving back to check over and over.

DRIPPING TAPS

Staring and staring for ages, wiping up each little drip until the tap stopped dripping. What if the house floods? It's my fault. Logic and my husband would say, 'Wendy, the water will go down the plughole', but no, the illogical always won. Taps in public toilets or places had to be checked and turned off over and over again. Waiting for people to leave, so I could turn them off perfectly to my way of thinking.

BREAD!!!

I had to have the perfect loaf of bread—the biggest, and straightest, with no dints. Checking each loaf on the shelf, feeling embarrassed by people looking at me, having to put the better loaves in my trolley, walk to an emptier aisle to recheck each over and over before making my selection, and feeling mentally exhausted.

I used to say 'IF ONLY I COULD BE FREE!' 'I just want to be free!'

I wish I had a broken leg instead—at least you can see that. It's something tangible and it will mend. You can't see a broken mind. A broken mind seems unmendable when one is feeling helpless and powerless. I felt no one understood. I desperately needed to be understood and accepted, have someone to talk to, have support and not feel alone. I was lonely in a private hell.

Things I found useful:

SELF ESTEEM
Learning about me, how I think, awareness of self and the way in which I respond and learn about the issues that affected my life.

VARIETY OF APPROACHES / THERAPY GROUPS
I benefited from being in a group—the bonding in the group was extremely helpful. There was trust, support, understanding and acceptance of each other, much laughter too and lasting friendships were forged in inspiring and empowering each other.

MINDFULNESS WORKSHOPS
Learning to live in the now and not to be preoccupied with the past or the future.

The good part of therapy is being able to take control of myself and make some of my own decisions, so I'm not being forced at a pace that isn't right for me—the therapist and the person living with OCD are a team.

People find it hard and rarely feel safe to articulate their feelings and thoughts. A good therapist listens to the first-hand life experiences of the person living with OCD. I know what's best for me, it's important for me that a therapist values and respects what I am saying and truly understands how OCD directly impacts on my life, and the people around me. And doesn't tell me what to do! That just defeats the purpose of me being empowered.

Being understood and being accepted for who you are and where you're at! Whoever and wherever that is!

ALBURY WODONGA SUPPORT GROUP

In a group you soon learn you are not alone or isolated. There are other people with familiar experiences and you know it's not just you. You feel safe in a non-judgemental environment.

These things helped me …

Humour—lots of laughs.

Time—working through this at my own pace.

Being honest with myself and others.

THE TURNING POINT

I feel blessed that things started to fall into place. They didn't change quickly. It has been a life-long journey—days, months, years and years … of discovering me.

Along my journey I found me, and I continue to find me! I saw my future travelling alongside others and helping, and at the same time being inspired. I have learnt a lot of things about myself. I have more self-belief and I know there is hope.

You know, I feel this journey was chosen for me, so that I could try to help others, just like I have been helped!

At a certain point I realised I felt like a tree! Wanting to be firmly connected to the ground but forever reaching upwards and outwards, sheltering others under my branches. We all lose leaves and dead wood, we grow new shoots, and we blossom and grow. I feel it's important for everyone to have faith and trust in oneself, to be kind and gentle to oneself, along with giving oneself rewards, and being our own best friend.

I have made many friends who are a special part of my life.

People who are recovering say that the people who believed in them when they did not believe in themselves, who encouraged their recovery but did not force it, who tried to listen and understand when nothing seemed to be making sense, were critical in their recovery. They needed to have someone that could be trusted to be there in times of need. It is strange, but in some ways I feel my suffering from OCD has eventually led to great gains in my life—experiencing what it is like to suffer, to truly feel fear, to have more understanding, compassion, and tolerance for others that I may not have had before. I have been able to find new meaning from my life with OCD by turning it into an experience that enables me now to help others.

JACOB

My mob is home. They know me, see me for me. I may have hurt them in the past but they're the only ones who will be there for me in the end.

I used to get really violent and then black out and that. Usually once or twice a week, mostly because of alcohol and drugs. Didn't worry me. My family said I had anger issues and needed to learn how to control myself. I was 17 when I was diagnosed with a mental disorder. I'm 27 now and been on and off my meds. Sometimes it's hard to keep up with them all, I'd rather not say what meds they are. I honestly can't remember most of the names of 'em! But when it did hit me that I had a mental illness, I got real depressed. I tried to harm myself a couple of times in different ways too. Stupid shit ya know? Pills, alcohol, reckless behaviour … I felt like my life was worthless and I'd never be able to live a normal and healthy one. I lashed out at my family, blaming them for my own mistakes. I even began to lash out at my own culture because of the stigma us mob get placed with, ay. I just wanted it all to end, the negativity and that.

It was hard enough being a young black male, where stereotypes that want you to fail already taint your own desires of being somebody. I'm a blackfella and proud too. I try not to think negative though anymore, it gets me down and sometimes even wild. I got ripped for all the bad shit I did by family and had to earn that respect back. Of course, they didn't know it was this thing in me that was causing most of my issues. At the time all the voices in my head were betraying me, telling me I'm nothing, just a down and out black who is like the rest. Society can do that to you though—they stereotype us, especially when you try living by your own cultural protocols and lore. Keeping a balance is harder than it looks. Most of us lose our way because of it; we live in two worlds of expectations. We cop the black politics among our own and the white politics that are forced upon us. Sorry for gettin' all political ay, I tend to do that when I'm anxious! I get anxiety sometimes and forget the point.

I am on my meds still, for my anxiety, anger, and my mind; there are a few that I think I'd have to get back to ya on, ay. These days I have regular check-ups and the family tries to keep me in line too. If I didn't have them, I'd be no one. That's the best thing about being a blackfella—no matter what you do or how fucked up your life may get you will always have your people, your home.

I can always say I am Jacob and I'm from the Yorta-Yorta mob and that. When you take a blackfella away from that and incarcerate them or lock them up in a rehab or clinic that's when you're nobody and things become harder to handle. A long time away from home can make you lonely. People think that all that stuff that happened in the past was then and we should move on. They miss the point altogether, it is because of the past most of us have issues living in society even functioning normal in a way that they see fit today. It still affects every generation like a cycle but we all handle it in our own way.

I'm a light-skinned blackfella and that used to mess with my head a bit, 'cause although I knew I was black at heart and in my spirit, people would only see the outside of me and assume I was half-caste or a whitefella. It wasn't until they got to know me, they'd find out my parents were black. If you are Aboriginal then it shouldn't matter how black you are or if you are a half-caste, quarter-caste. That's bullshit! I don't ask every white Australian if they are half British because of their ancestry; they believe themselves to be true blue Aussies. So why am I or any other blackfella treated differently? I'm sorry to ramble, my head is running a mile a minute.

My mob is home. They know me, see me for me. I may have hurt them in the past but they're the only ones who will be there for me in the end. That's how I've managed this 'illness', they call it, as long as I keep positive and that I know I'll survive. I guess some blackfellas can get ousted if they've done wrong but that comes down to tribal punishment, and they'd have to do something really wrong within the whole community.

For someone who is suffering an illness like me, most of the time the mob are just as scared as you 'bout it. Because it can be unpredictable with your actions and you don't exactly get educated in mental health unless you choose to do health. I think this can cause a stigma in community and leave you isolated.

Once the mob begins to understand through those information sessions and workshops that the local co-op sometimes has, then fellas get used to it and don't hold it against you. Everyone, especially the aunties and uncles make sure you're OK. Usually I just let people know if I'm having a good day or a bad day. When I have a bad day, it's hard to get out of bed, so I stay home. Mob will visit me if they don't see me out and about, make sure I'm all right. I did stay at the clinic the first week, I think of my diagnosis, so they could monitor me and assess my issues, for a few days. But I was released under the care of my uncle and aunt—they keep an eye on me.

I do my best to stay away from the alcohol and so far I'd say I'm better because of it. I don't touch drugs no more, but if I didn't mix my yarndi with other drugs, I'd probably be still smoking it. It's less lethal than these cancer sticks everyone's hooked on, including myself. The mixing of drugs and alcohol fuelled my issues, cos that's when the violent outbursts and voices in my head began ya know. Negative and nasty spirits in this mind—those memories push me to not be that person anymore. As long I keep takin' these drugs they prescribed me and stay on a track that's stable, I'll survive.

A good day is when I'm up early, whistlin' in the shower to oldies like Charley Pride and Slim Dusty. That music makes me peaceful and I think of the old fellas who played 'em when I was a kid. That gets me started and in a good mood. Then it's smiles all day and I'm social. I'll visit everybody when I'm having a good day.

Work is casual at the moment but it feels good to be working, ay. Just doing some labour here and there even for the old people is good, makes me feel like I'm giving back to the community and keeps me sane. Right now, the co-op has me maintaining the lawns and gardens for our Elders, and I love it.

It's taken me four years to finally get used to it, the meds and that. I wanna show our next generation who may be strugglin' that even though you have some heavy shit going on and you may feel like lashing out at the world, you will always have your mob there to get you through it. I try to tell them there is more to life and they should go out and live it the best way they can, whether they have an illness like mine or not.

CREATIVITY

CREATIVITY

Photo by David Rennie, titled 'Near Miss', which won the prestigious
ANZANG Nature Photographer of the Year award in 2013.

BIRD WATCHER

by Natasha Rubinstein from an interview with
D A V I D   R E N N I E

Sitting by the lake absorbing the sunshine of Mandurah sits a bird watcher, an artist, a woodworker, a photographer, an insomniac and a father. The man is David. David has bipolar disorder. His life, like many others, has been coloured by achievement and pleasure, pain and suffering. He differs from the 'norm' in that his projects fill him to overflowing with creativity and single-mindedness. His low phases are equally as extreme, as he isolates himself in the bush to recuperate for days or weeks.

His ventures consume him; he'd paint 20 paintings in a row when he was invested in painting, and stay in the bush for days photographing numerous birds of different species when that became his fixation. He started a successful woodwork business and eventually had 20 people working with him, until he was incapable of continuing. He started photography in 2007, after spotting an interesting looking bird he could not identify. He bought his first camera and went out into the swamp to photograph more birds. He fell in love with the swamp's isolation and beauty, and described photographing there as an 'uncontrollable love affair'. He was soon completely consumed by his addiction to photography. During this phase, David wouldn't sleep for weeks on end and became dependent on photography for his survival in many ways.

But he took his last nature photograph in 2010. During a low phase he got frustrated and deleted hundreds of thousands of photos 'because I went dark, didn't want to do it anymore'.

David is a unique bipolar sufferer, in the sense that eleven out of twelve months of the year he goes through manic phases and episodes. He will rarely sleep during these phases, and then hibernate for long periods when the low phase begins. During manic phases, there can be a distortion between reality and fantasy and an impulsivity that has significantly contributed to David's life. 'I once fell 40 feet off a cliff and just laughed', he recalls. His mania controls his sleeping patterns, passions, and family life. He constantly needs to keep going and going until his mania temporarily lapses.

David is fortunate to be surrounded by a loving family, and he seeks solace in serene and beautiful nature. The seclusion of the bush provides him with much-needed space during the low phases, and a calming space in which to experience the darker times.

David shuns the standard notion of normal, the passionless life devoted to a nine-to-five job to pay the bills, and instead devotes his life to his inspirations. The widely accepted definition of normal isn't necessarily better, and David is living proof of that. He managed to 'come out of the dark with determination'. Thus, he treats every day as a day of wonderment, where anything could happen.

David has a rather unique take on his mental illness, 'It's wonderful. I'm sad everyone doesn't have it, they don't get to see and do things the way I experience them. I love it. It's all I've known, I know no different.'

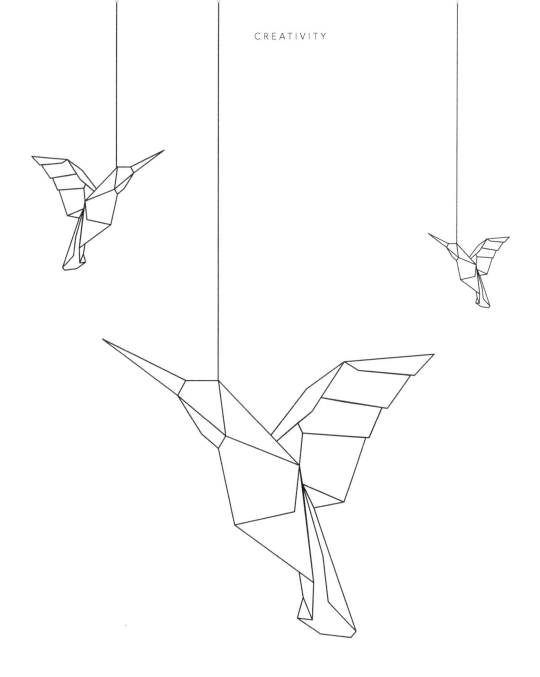

WE HAVE PUSHED AWAY ART

M I C   E A L E S

We have pushed away art, fantasy, stories, traditions and
spirituality from our books and our clinical rooms ... giving
way to formulas and rationalism. In doing so, we have deprived
science of its human experience and true soul.
~ ERMINIA COLUCCI

I was in Barcelona for a conference. For part of it I dressed as Magritte's surrealist painting 'The Son of Man' (bowler hat and hanging apple) and did a performance piece called 'An Arts-Based Response to Suicide' in which I wrote the numbers 1 through to 3000 in crayon across my PhD, which I had printed onto four pianola scrolls. I then displayed it along the ornate black and white tiled passageway. Why? Because one person every 30 seconds takes their own life. That's about 3000 every day.

The silence surrounding suicide exists because suicide exposes and challenges our humanness. To find ways to breach this silence and to research and talk about the issue, I try to engage with people through art. My interest is in how art, like writing the numbers 1–3000, can poetically embody the voice of suicide while instilling a sense of hope and an embracing of life.

My immediate reaction on hearing of my brother Bryan's suicide in September 2002 was, 'That bastard, he succeeded and I failed!'

As a child, I was the dreamer of the two, lost in a world of fantasy; I was shy, withdrawn, sensitive and insecure. I loved nothing more than playing in the dirt and wearing out the knees of my pants. But when my parents moved from the open spaces of an outback sheep station I began a new claustrophobic life in the suburbs.

When I was 9 we played a kissing game with the girls across the road. It ended with the younger brother of one of them whipping me with a length of garden hose and everyone laughing. I felt far more than humiliation. I withdrew more and more into myself and then began self-harming. I felt so small and weak.

I hated school and one day I took to my knee with a lump of wood, repeatedly hitting it to the point where I couldn't walk. I poured boiling water over my hands. It would be far easier to explain these actions if I had I been bullied at school, but in all honesty I simply did not feel as if I belonged. There was some form of perverse enjoyment and satisfaction in seeing my flesh open up as I began cutting myself and observing my inner pain, oozing out, along with the blood.

I experienced my first suicidal crisis when I was 15. Positioning a rifle barrel in my mouth, I was about to pull the trigger when my parents walked past the kitchen window. I panicked. I couldn't do it to them and I hid the rifle before they entered the house. No one ever knew of my deeply intense pyschological pain.

My art studio is an outer reflection of my chaotic inner world. As you walk towards the building the first thing you notice is the cluttered mess. Recycled timber is stacked up outside, a pile of river stones forms a sort of cairn next to some old broken timber windows and frames. Inside, plaster and rubber moulds lay piled on benches, aluminium road signs lean up against steel shelving, which in turn lean up against drums of casting materials. The cluttered-ness and mess on the studio floor, along with the disarray of benches filled with tools and sticks of oil paint, cannot be avoided. For all of its turmoil and unruliness there is a sense of order, that someone who uses this space comprehends the gist of it all.

Today I looked at the acid burns still visible on my hands. They are a constant reminder of a time when I couldn't stand being me, a time when the physical pain of being burnt helped alleviate the deeply emotional pain of living. It is so ironic that today I use acid in the patination process in my studio, to bring alive my bronze sculptures.

Just after my 18th birthday I tried to take my own life once again, this time with pills and alcohol. I woke up the next morning having vomited the pills up some time during the night. Again, no one ever knew and I wasn't about to confess, at least not for several years.

As a child I had thought of entering a career in the Church for a fulfilled life. But in Sunday School one day, it was said that anyone who had not been baptised would go to hell. My parents had decided not to have me baptised; they wanted me to make that decision when and if I chose to do so. My vision of a life serving God and humanity was now in question. Yes, I could get baptised and my problem would be solved, but my concern was not for myself but for all of the other souls—the men, women and particularly children, who had lived before me and who had never heard about Christianity, let alone the practice of baptism. Were they all in hell? It made me question everything and if or where I belonged.

My hope is that through my artwork, the stories of suicide and people's ability to live inspired lives after such an attempt will encourage greater understanding and empathy for the suicidal mind and help to unlock some of its mysteries.

In China some years ago, I collected lotus pods for an artwork in an attempt to draw attention to suicide among women in rural China. As I was collecting the pods, I was struck by the two worlds that I was immersed in. Above the water were these exquisite flowers, magnificent water-repelling broad leaves and tall spires thrusting these joyous pods towards the heavens. However, as I began to sink deeper into the muddy depths of the pond with the water rising almost to my shoulders, I was made aware of another darker, more primordial, world. It is little wonder that the lotus features so prominently as a symbol of life and spirituality in so many cultures.

In remembrance of those that we have lost to suicide, a small group of us attending an international suicide prevention conference scattered the 100 or so pods that I collected into a canal near the convention centre's entrance.

As we did this, I said, 'I ask you to reflect on how you might bring some joy, hope and inspiration, not only into your own lives but also into the lives of those you love, into the lives of your colleagues and even into the lives of strangers.'

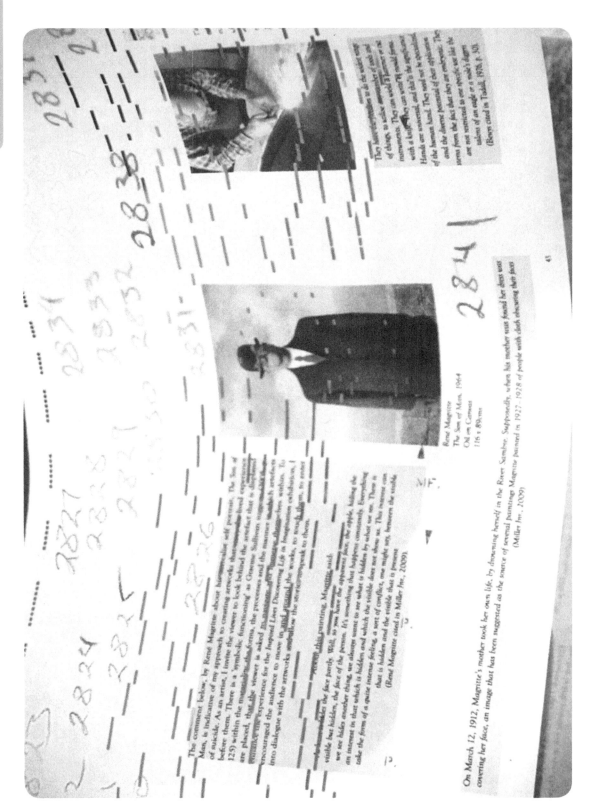

Magritte's Imposter—Mic Eales. Barcelona Performance

Magritte's Imposter—Mic Eales. Melbourne Performance

THE BOOK OF NICE THINGS

AMY SPURLING

She makes notes on nice things.

Birdsong, smiles ...

Part of her mindfulness and meditation, staying present.

If you've felt sadness on the inside—like an empty shell, on an egg-shells floor,

like you're moving through mud and you can't stop crying and you want to sleep

forever, suicidal—

it's not just life.

It's real.

She's spreading the word.

She's got a brave face on, she's so brave in this battle with no middle and no end.

Meditation, medication.

And emotional regulation:

separate the rational from the irrational.

What's in your Book of Nice Things?

Jacaranda carpet, azalea fireworks, magnolia chandeliers.

And acts of kindness.

A MOUTHFUL

K I A H   M E A D O W S

*This is my creative non-fiction piece about my own experience
suffering from severe social anxiety that presented itself a lot like
bulimia. This happened to me earlier this year and I'm still trying
to work through it. This piece was written in the thick of things.*

In the classroom I sit in my usual chair that spins and creaks the love of my life is in this room I think I feel sick. One of the loves I still feel sick.

'Have you eaten?' I am embarrassed yes I have eaten and I will eat again I don't want to talk about this now or ever.

The library doesn't have the film that it says it has. I bite my apple and throw it away I feel too hot and too tired I feel anxious I am hovering around myself and dead weight in the hall I bend over the toilet and stick my fingers down my throat.

I sit at home alone and watch *Dancer in the Dark* and eat spaghetti bolognaise I'm not sure if the meat is too old to be eaten by a human being. I hear my Nan and my teacher and my friend and Deneuve in my head telling me 'this is unnecessary I hate that movie he is an idiot she is so whiny that role wasn't really meaty enough for me' I force two heaping bowls of pasta into my mouth and out again.

It smells of incense and curry and it feels a little bit like I've stepped into another dimension or reality. The girls are sweet and we talk superficially about school and life and dance around the subjects of cancer and MS.

'My Mum's fine, how's your Mum, fine?'

I hope they don't look at me eating because it's good and I eat fast and Lis has seconds I'm full and so very happy that I'm full and she ate more than I did.

We all have a fight on Facebook about what the rules are for the thing we created together. These people are my friends and I don't want them to hate me already I don't even know if they like me now I eat my sandwich and my apple and some biscuits and I swallow all my water although it resists we meet in an emergency coming together of voices and ideas and I feel insignificant and unsure of my place am I blushing am I staring am I too loud in the stall?

I eat a biscuit at 4.45 I have to be at Meg's by 6. At 5 I throw up my biscuit. I talk at people I don't know and people I thought I knew but I'm not so sure anymore about the fact that they don't go to university and they have a full time job and I don't know what to say because I'm a not-quite-published freelance journalist who's not a journalist and lives at home and goes to university. At 8.50 I throw up my dinner. Dad drives me home because I don't drive either and neither one of us knows what to say because what do you say? At 9.30 I throw up in the comfort of my own home.

My therapist asks how I've been doing and I ramble on about how I'm doing so well at school and I have wonderful friends and I'm getting good grades and I really love it and how I wrote a piece about my dad that was scary to write 'Why?' because people won't like me if they know that 'Not everybody's going to like you' that's a horrible thing to say! Let's talk about my father. I think of the people and that one person I want to like me and my stomach growls as I tell her I don't think my father likes me and nothing else.

I have to tell my doctor that I do it to myself but I don't control it 'It's hard to be at school and I don't want the pills to make me feel sick.' I don't want the pills to affect my ability to orgasm like the last ones but I wouldn't tell him that or anyone ever and now I won't be depressed or anxious or throw up anymore I go to the public toilet and stick my shaking fingers as far back as they will go and I scratch my throat with my nails and my nose runs and my eyes water.

I write a short film without dialogue about a bad thing that happened to someone else that wasn't me I promise. I wrote it before I realized that I do the same thing and am now embarrassed that I wrote it I won't let my mum read it I wont tell the people who have read it about my thing.

Mum asks me how I'm feeling and what I ate she asks me if I've thrown up today. Now that she's watching me I feel like it's all my fault and I'm doing something wrong but I can't help it it's like breathing I hide my greed and go to bed hungry but full but not full enough to throw up and therefore still hungry. I wake up famished and on the phone to my grandmother I finish my cereal she talks a lot but this time I talk more than she does I can't say I'll call you back Nan after another bowl of cereal and I've gotten rid of it so I'm hungry-full-nauseous a new feeling that I hate.

I have to read my piece to the class I don't have to I chose to and I don't know if it's because I'm a masochist a perfectionist or I crave attention or all of the above. I feel nervous and don't want to go first but at the same time I know it's good so I'm not too worried people like it a lot and I am overjoyed that they like it my fingers and my knees shake. I feel sick but can't feel better yet I buy two cookies before I get on the train and I know what is going to happen when I eat them both within five minutes it's not that I want it to happen but it will make me feel better I throw up and I know that people in the other stalls can hear me gag and cough and I feel so so tired afterwards I go to bed at eight proud of my positive feedback.

I feel tense like I'm in pain or guilty when she's there that I feel the way I do I laugh at the jokes no more and no less than anyone else is I visit the back alley bathroom I visit the in-the-back-room bathroom and the 3:00am bathroom because I dreamed about disappointing her I go to the hospital because it's debilitating. I think about her and the hum of the globes and the wailing of patients and the vent that killed my grandfather with its diseases in this hospital 15 years ago another wave of nausea washes over me but people are looking so I can't throw up and I feel silly talking about it so I just keep on staring at the vent until I can't see the vent or the ceiling or her face in my mind's eye.
The new pills make me more aware than I was about my feelings for others and nothing

to do with them and my gut churns. 'What are you going to tell her?' I can feel the acid rising in my throat as I watch her take her shirt off in front of me my friend not a woman not an object of desire. The feelings come back should I leave now or should I stay? As she leans in to read I look up from my page at the swell of her breast overflowing from her bra beneath her satin shirt and my leg twitches reminding me to look down and breathe deep and hold in my lunch and don't say a word.

I have a cup of tea and write about this eating disorder or stomach ulcer social anxiety or whatever the fuck this means and hesitate before I reach into my mouth only because of the sour assault that I get from my tongue on my dry skin. I throw up my tea and reasonable sized lunch and return to my writing with clean hands that still manage to smell like bile and a sore red knuckle on my middle finger from my two crooked front teeth.

ART AND TRAUMA, LOSS AND GRIEF

A N N E   R I G G S

'Like the clay, she said, women seem soft, malleable and weak. Like clay being made durable by the firing process, those who have survived extreme tension find they too have remarkable resilience and strength.'

Many people who have been abused find it very difficult to express their feelings of hurt, anger, confusion, desire for revenge and pain. These are all hard to put into words; expressing feelings of anger and desire for revenge can also cause great harm if they are not expressed in a healthy way.

Nonetheless, most professionals would agree that it is important for victims of abuse to be able to express the full range of their emotions and to acknowledge the situations in which these feelings arose.

Art is one way of expressing these important and deep feelings without causing harm to either the survivor or others. Women who have participated in our art groups have told me that expressing feelings in art—especially clay—has been really useful to them. They have found that their feelings 'go through their fingers and into the clay' and they are able to see in their art works the feelings that have been hard to express in words.

'My journey to the art group—the last place you'd expect to find me. I've died so many times, in so many ways along this journey. My demons descend, tormenting. A tortured soul, so fragile, haunted with fear. Painful memories from the past cloud my mind relentlessly. The art group—a time to travel deep within myself. My screams are silenced. There are no rules here. No expectations. No one fails. My fears are calmed. Alone, but yet there is a connectedness to others. A place to belong, waking me softly as I sit in the present. A blank canvass is all I see. This is my chance to be just me. Emotions are dancing, I am actually alive. A masterpiece I have been hiding inside. Those eyes closed tight can actually see. Not a word is spoken—the art tells my story.'

— Valerie (an art group participant and childhood sexual assault survivor)

One way of expressing emotions is to work with different materials—such as clay, paper, wire, fabric and nails – in such a way that each will change in the kiln. We know that the clay will become stronger, the paper and fabric will burn away leaving only ash, and the wire and nails will become brittle. These changes offer a visual language to express strength, frailty, endurance, tension and resilience.

Participants can use the wire and nails quite viciously in the wet clay at the same time as knowing that they will become brittle through firing. Perhaps that can help express the anger—then allow a process for that feeling to become less intense? One woman created a home environment using a range of materials. It seemed to tell a story of her childhood and feelings of entrapment and insecurity. But when it was fired, the cage became fragile. Although she still feels the impact of abuse, as an adult she is perhaps acknowledging that she is not as disempowered as she was as a child.

'I had only told my secret about a year ago, before the mosaic class began. I thought people would be talking about the abuse, and I'd never gone in to the details, as I feel like I am betraying my father and the secret I thought would go to the grave with me.

I had trouble doing mosaics as I thought it had to be perfect. And I would hear my dad's voice in my head that it wasn't good enough, and that I was hopeless and stupid. Even people in the class would say my work was good but I didn't believe them, and thought they were just saying that to be nice. The first piece I hated so much I gave it away to someone. I had way too much expectation on myself that could get in the way. To this day I still have trouble cutting and get frustrated.

One project was on how we see ourselves. My piece was dark—I had the devil in the background, representing my hatred towards myself and my father. Then there was a dove flying, with a bit of sun and blue sky over the devil, which represented the hope of having peace one day with myself and having acceptance of what had happened to me. It took me ages to finish this piece as it would bring up a lot of emotions. I had never dealt with my feelings, and would block it out with alcohol and drugs. There were times that I was so depressed I started drinking and couldn't make it to class as I was in a psych ward, detox or parks. But I've managed to finally clean up my act and hope that by doing the mosaic class again, that the pieces that I am doing now will not affect me.'

—Simone (a survivor of sexual assault who has struggled with substance abuse for many years, but through mosaics has found a way to express her deep emotions)

The art groups are a special part of all our weeks. Participants are never asked to reveal or disclose anything about their past or present experiences, although some choose to share some elements of their stories. As they learn to express themselves through their art the focus of these groups is creative practice and not therapy. Themes around the self, the past, baggage, the body and the future help participants look at themselves and their lives with different eyes. The magical thing about these groups is the sense of community that grows and holds women safely as each tries new creative practices, using these to express something of her inner life.

I work with women and families who are affected by abuse at the South Eastern Centre Against Sexual Assault and at Connections Uniting Care, and ran a men's group with the Northern Centre Against Sexual Assault, in Melbourne. A recurring theme in the men's group has been how to work out which aspects of life's challenges are a result of their abuse history, and which are just part of the rough and tumble that all of us face and have to deal with. It is a challenging question and one that inspired much discussion and contemplation.

Most of the men were abused between the ages of 8 and 14, some by family members, others through people associated with school and church. All the experiences have left life-long scars. Abuse affects how survivors relate to others, how their education and therefore work life unfolds, how individuals feel about themselves—their self-worth and how they feel about others. As a result, trust can be difficult to establish and maintain. Additional to the many and profound effects of abuse that both men and women experience, men have additional layers to contend with such as societal beliefs/fears to contend with that relate to sexuality and a male victim's potential to grow up and harm others. These last two fears can further silence male victims.

TINY SPARTAN WARRIOR

This clay piece represents the need I have to wear armour. It wasn't for protection against the abuse, it was for protection against people knowing.

My abuse started with bullying and, as is fairly typical, this wasn't taken seriously by those who I tried to tell. My parents were more concerned by damaged uniforms than by the bruises I had. When they did complain to the school, the principle would yell at the grade and give a couple of them token punishments like lines or a lunchtime detention. Once or twice they got the cane but that was rare. As soon as they finished their punishments, they took it out on me for dobbing. One time a teacher really pressured me into telling her what was upsetting me so much and when I blurted it out I got a detention for the language I used and told that they were willing to listen when I was prepared to discuss it in a mature way.

It became obvious to me that telling was the best way I knew of getting hurt more. It therefore became imperative that I hid the evidence. I had to develop an entire personality in order to do this. I have come to call this personality my armour.

Outwardly I was active, funny and easy going. That was the armour at work.
But it took so much effort to turn off the pain and act like nothing was wrong.
The act of putting the armour on was as bad as anything that was being done
to me and it took all my effort just to wear it.

This piece is a reflection of how much strength is needed to just wear the armour.
It is far too big for the child. This is my way of showing that someone
else should have been wearing it for him.

—Stuart Murphy (participant in the Northern CASA Men's Art group)

If they feel comfortable I invite men and women who have experienced sexual abuse to share their creative reflections for the benefit of others who may have experienced abuse also. It is in this sharing that healing can happen, silence can be broken and some deeper understanding gained.

I am amazed sometimes by the work that emerges from under the fingertips of those who have suffered trauma, but in many ways, I am not. I know each of us has great potential to be creative. I also know that each participant in our art groups, or groups all over the world has great potential to step out from the shadow of their unhappy past to create a sense of wellbeing for themselves and others.

Anne Riggs is a visual artist, researcher and trainer who recieved a PhD from Victoria University, Melbourne for research into the effects of arts practice on recovery after trauma, loss and grief (sexual abuse) and a Master of Fine Arts from the Victorian College of the Arts, Melbourne for research into the artist's response into the impacts of the First World War. She has built much of her creative life upon the artist's role in expressing and responding to the most profound human experiences.

Please visit www.anneriggs.com for more information on the art classes and stories of participants, and to read her thesis:
The Creative Space. Art in the Shadow of Trauma, Loss and Grief.

The 'Message in a Bottle' video project on Anne's website (and how Valerie and Simone share their stories) was funded by the South Eastern Centre Against Sexual Assault (Melbourne) with a grant from the Victorian Women's Trust. If you need to speak with a sexual assault counsellor please phone 1800 806 292 (Victoria) or 1800 737 732 (Australia Wide).

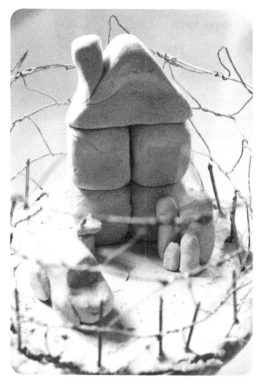 

House Sculpture: *Created by a woman participant of a SECASA (South Eastern Centre Against Sexual Assault) group, 2013. This young woman was sexually abused by a relative. The sculpture explores that environment, and also works with the knowledge that the wire will weaken and break in the firing—in a sense, her cage is broken by art.*

Bowl: *Created by a female participant of a SECASA (South Eastern Centre Against Sexual Assault) group, 2013.*

FEAR AND LOATHING

LIZ MCSHANE

Wearing nothing but a paper gown, Xandra stared at the ceiling of the Dr Gambi & Associates Wellness Centre treatment room and counted backwards, trying to ignore the tugging on her right ankle as Nurse Charlie tightened the last remaining strap. With the exception of a cracked and faded sun flower painting, which Xandra was taught to focus on when she was a child, the ceiling was otherwise a stark white canvas. She strained her eyes to look across at the two-way mirror; she wondered what it would be like to stand on the other side of that mirror and watch while a little girl, scared and alone, cried for her parents.

Just Like Me by Liz McShane. Unpublished.

At a writer's conference last year something that struck a chord occurred during one of the Q&As. I can't remember which panel it was, but, as per usual, an audience member asked the panellists how they dealt with writer's block. One of the panellists made reference to the writer and depression, but said it was separate from writer's block and the conversation moved on. I was not ready to move on.

I have endured bouts of depression and anxiety since my early teens. For most of my young adult life I assumed that was the way things were—I was and would forever be a paranoid pessimist whose mind was often flooded with so many layers of unending and indistinguishable self-loathing thoughts that they became indecipherable, leaving me with nothing but a heavy numbness in my head. Writing allowed me to immerse myself in characters and stories far removed from my own reality. But, in 2010 my mother died and the grief process turned into a bleak and intensely paranoid state of being that endured long after the first anniversary of her death, and in the midst of it all my writing stopped. Completely. I assumed that I was experiencing grief that would pass at some point, but still made an appointment with my GP. She gently pointed out my family history of anxiety and depression (putting a name to what I previously assumed were aspects of my personality) and then she said something that blew my mind—'you shouldn't have to feel like this'. I saw a hypnotherapist, counsellor, psychologist and psychiatrist, all of whom helped me realise (well, maybe not the hypnotherapist) that what I had been experiencing all those years, even prior to my mother dying, was not, and did not have to be, a part of my personality. I learned to identify when I was on the verge of a high-anxiety episode, or when I was falling into a state of depression. With their assistance, I put tools in place to combat negative thoughts with positive, rational self-talk. This doesn't mean I always win. I am a work in progress. What it does mean, is that while depression and anxiety do not define who I am, I have accepted that depression and anxiety will always be a part of my life that I need to manage.

Getting actively involved in the writing community is the best thing I can do for my own writing and my ongoing battle with depression and anxiety. It's extremely difficult but listening to artists talk about their hardships proved equally as inspiring to me as listening to them talk about their successes.

Libba Bray, an American YA writer, was one of the most captivating panellists I listened to at the conference last year. Libba also blogs openly about her battle with depression and her life as an author dealing with it. 'There appears to be a large correlation between artists and depression. But I would argue that artistic expression is not a symptom of depression so much as a response to it. I see writing as an act of resistance against an occupying enemy who means to kill me,' she says.

After the conference I was more determined than ever to get back into writing, I just didn't know how to break through the crippling nothingness caused by my anxiety and depression. I signed up for NaNoWriMo, an online community where writers are challenged with writing a 50,000-word manuscript in a month. I decided to use this challenge to re-write my YA manuscript, *Just Like Me*, which had been sitting on the shelf doing nothing for well over a year. To succeed at this challenge I would have to write 1667 words per day. There was no time to second-guess ideas before they made it to the page. There was no time to delete chapters, pages, paragraphs or sentences. To begin with, it was the all too quick passing of time and the measly word count chartered on my NaNoWriMo account page that forced me to write. Then, the camaraderie with co-workers who took up the challenge and the enthusiasm of other co-workers who constantly asked for progress reports motivated me to keep going. Finally, a creative flow carried me through to the end, and I completed the challenge with a few days to spare. While some polishing and additional writing was required, my manuscript benefited greatly from the experience, as being time poor forced my inner pessimist to the side, allowing creativity to thrive.

Maybe I won't ever be a published novelist, but I've benefited greatly from hearing the ups and downs of other writers, and I hope that blogging about my own journey as a writer fumbling through (and hopefully, at some point, thriving in) the Melbourne literary scene will help other like-minded artists to do the same.

Excerpts and text taken from the blog posts of Liz McShane:
lizkatemcshane.wordpress.com and Libba Bray: libbabray.wordpress.com

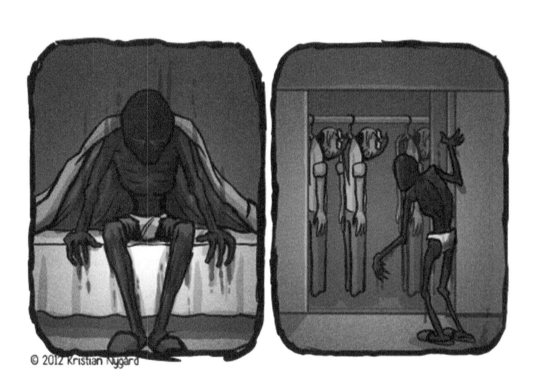

© 2012 Kristian Nygård

SOUL FIRE STARTER

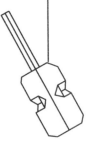

HEIDI EVERETT

Mental illness is not the experience; it's the way you deal with it.

My name's Heidi E and I'm a Mental Health Wrangler and Soul Fire Starter. I'm not a health professional or a weird crackpot on a kooky trip. I'm simply a normal person who lives with a mental illness called schizo-affective disorder (which basically means I have a big scoop of schizy mixed with many generous doses of major depression).

Mental Sk'illness is a simple and honest way of reconnecting with yourself through your own unique passions, interests and personal belief systems. It celebrates that living with a mental illness doesn't mean you need to focus just on the negative stuff. It's about the ability to find positives in living with a mental illness.

Psychiatry can often overrule the wonderful person you are underneath the illness, and we can easily forget about ourselves, especially if we're told too often that we are sick and need to get better.

A man on the street once stopped me with his musical strumming. The beauty of his music inspired me to learn classical guitar and it brought back the verve of life. Now, as an established songwriter years later, I wrote lyrics about holding on. Because if you've ever experienced the long, lonely nights in an episode, you know how bloody hard it is to get through til the next morning. In those times I have to remind myself a) to aim for the sunrise, b) to hold on to the things/people that I love and c) I've been here before and I survived.

But when the sun comes up in the morning, that's what I'm aiming for,
I'm holding on to the best things of my life.
And when the sun comes up in the morning, that's when I know I've been here before,
I'm holding on to the best things of my life.

Mental illness gives you many stripes to wear proudly on your shoulder. Some of these are: persistence, tenacity, intelligence, patience, empathy, tolerance, inspiration, bravery, curiosity, a sense of humour, perception, appreciation.

If you've never had to fight for your rights, your mind and your life, you will not have had to develop such a remarkable set of exceptional tools to experience this world as it's meant to be experienced.

In my song called Running Away I say:

> *I don't want to be afraid any more, I want to see it all come true.*
> *I've had enough of seeing the world, now I want to be in it too.*

Because, enough of being characterised by mental illness, whatever shape or form it takes. Enough with taking a backseat and being a soul passenger—get yourselves up the front and start driving!

Useful street language for mental illness:
MI—mental illness
schizy—schizophrenia
BP—bipolar
funky philosopher's hotel—psyche ward
yep—I completely zoned out while you were talking and didn't hear a word you said

Text excerpts taken from www.skillness.org. For more information
on Mental Sk'illness, Heidi's current projects or to download her tunes,
please visit www.heidieverett.com.au.

RUBBER DUCK ON A ROUGH SEA

FIONA SAWYER
member of SANE Australia's Board of Directors

Diagnosed with generalised anxiety disorder, it wasn't until later in life that I began to see the connection between my depression and feelings of excessive anxiety. Suddenly it made complete sense. I needed to ward off the anxiety in order to stop becoming depressive.

When I fell pregnant and was unable to take anti-depressant medication, I decided it was an opportunity to concentrate on psychotherapy instead.

The tools I have learnt to manage anxiety are amazing.

In one exercise I visualise my anxiety as a rubber duck riding a rough sea, which dissipates as calm returns. Now if I feel anxious, instead of trying to analyse the feeling I just stay with it and ride over the waves—like the rubber duck.

As I learned to cope with my anxiety through psychotherapy I went back to work and became an active member on the Board of SANE Australia. This was a position I was offered after organising a successful fundraising initiative in Sydney to support its work. SANE is independent and an organisation that is making a difference today. I highly value the fact that it focuses on improving understanding of mental illness.

Adapted from Fiona's Snapshot story on the SANE website: www.sane.org. SANE Australia is a national charity helping all Australians affected by mental illness lead a better life—through campaigning, education and research. Please see their website for more details, resources or to make a valuable donation.

HIGHWAYMAN

CATHERINE CAMDEN-PRATT

When I was twelve years old, Mum was living with us, during one of her 'good' periods. By the mid 1950s, Electro Convulsive Treatment had become the next new thing. Mum had more than her fair share of it and, after my brother was born, was one of the early recipients of Cardiazol, the chemical precursor to ECT. I remember how much Mum hated shock treatment, how it fried her brain. She came into my bedroom, I held my breath, she was trying to remember lines to one of her favourite poems. I would will her onto the next line, watching her jagged movement in and out of my bedroom doorway, her hands trying to wash the words into existence: 'The wind was a torrent of darkness among the gusty trees/ The moon was a ... the moon was ... the moon was a ... The wind was a torrent of darkness among the gusty trees/ The moon was a ... the moon was ... was a ... was ... was ... Cathy, the moon was a ... the moon was a ... what was the moon, Cathy?' 'The moon was a ghostly galleon, Mum.' 'That's right, it's the dammed shock treatment, I can't remember a thing, The wind was a torrent of darkness among the gusty trees/ The moon was a ghostly galleon tossed upon cloudy seas/ The road was a ... The road ... the road was a ... was a ... the road was ... Cathy, the road was a ... the road was a ... what was the road, Cathy?' 'The road was a ribbon of moonlight over the purple moor, Mum.' 'That's right, The wind was a torrent of darkness among the gusty trees/ The moon was a ... was a ... The moon was a ghostly galleon tossed upon cloudy seas/ The road was a ... the road was a ... was a ... Cathy what was the road?' It used to take hours—sometimes it was The Highwayman, sometimes it was Tarantella (despite her despairing of rhyming as a poetic device, which she thought Hilaire Beloc shamelessly overused), sometimes a line she couldn't identify from Shelley or Keats or Wordsworth. Sometimes it could take a whole night. I was glad my mother loved poetry. I was glad helping her helped me remember lines of poems I came to love. I was glad I found a relationship here with her in our jagged remembering of her favourite poems.

Catherine Camden Pratt has written a PhD thesis and a book about her mother's 'madness', and that of other women and mothers.
Daughters of Persephone: legacies of maternal 'madness' (2003) is a digital thesis available online at University of Western Sydney, and Out of the shadows: daughters growing up with a 'mad' mother, Finch Publications 2006.

Brisbane Lesbian and Gay Pride Choir. Photos by Tjeerd Tijhof

SHELTER

D A V I D   H A R D Y

There's this line in a song my choir performs, 'May you
always be our shelter, may we always live in peace.'
It's an Eric Bogle lyric that lingers.

Following New York's riots of 1969, the voices of gay, lesbian, bisexual, transgendered and intersex people were raised in song by the first of many such choirs, the Stonewall Chorale. It wasn't long before others emerged across North America and Europe, then Australia, reaching my home of Brisbane in 1998.

Some new members in my choir wear their queer identity on their sleeve, proudest when singing songs of protest and looking to make every performance count. Some wear their trauma tightly, bound up in their struggle with straightstream thinking. Identity crises in childhood, as teenagers or as adults leave them shell-shocked. It often takes time, months or a year or two, with the choir for them to feel peace. For a few, even a choir of people who get you is still too much, and they leave and come back but then leave again. For most, it becomes home.

One singer spoke to me about his life and what the choir means to him.

'Early on, and even later, I knew it wasn't safe to be gay. I knew homosexuality was considered bad so I didn't feel it was safe to reach out to anybody for fear of being beaten up or ostracised. I was scared of people finding out about who and what I was. So the safest thing for me was to shut down. I didn't have many friends.'

Anxiety and depression are labels he uses to talk about difficult times since his childhood. He had considered joining the choir for a while but was worried about his singing experience and wasn't sure if he would enjoy himself. He points to three reasons why he decided to come along to the first rehearsal.

'I always wanted to be a singer. I idolised Madonna when I was a kid and Kylie a bit later. If I couldn't be a singer, I thought I would happily fall in love and be a housewife, house husband, whatever.

'The second reason was that the choir was gay. And I figured the safest, most supportive place to learn something new would be amongst people who were also gay. Yes, there was a third reason: to meet someone. Most of the socialising I do in the gay community is about finding love. That's what it's about and the singing is a bonus.'

He tells me how big an effort it took to attend his first rehearsal.

'I reached out when I was most depressed, when all my dreams had disappeared. I was unemployed, I was isolated and lonely, drinking too much, smoking too much, generally not taking care of myself. That first night I was really scared about going, including about having rehearsals in a church, like we did back then. But as soon as I got there and realised it was safe and it was okay, that was it.

'Early on, there were still days I thought I can't face these people, I'm too depressed, too anxious, but I convinced myself this was one thing I could do, that the people were fine, that I didn't need to sing in pitch but I needed to be with people and that I would feel better by doing that.'

The Choir became his way of building a life back again.

'I've had a lot of different jobs. I've been in workplaces where the culture is really scary, where you are not game to talk about who you are and your sexuality. Choir is not like that. I feel like I can be myself, that I am not judged, that I don't have to worry about what other people think. It's a relief to be around people with similar interests, similar understandings, similar experiences. I mean everybody is still different, there's still diversity, but I can relax and be myself. And not worry about being gay. It's not an issue. It no longer becomes 'a thing'. Like everywhere else I go being gay is part of my identity and it is something I have to explain to people or people don't understand or it's a divide or a gap or an extra piece of distance, whereas in choir it becomes a non-issue. Yeah, we joke and talk and laugh in the choir as we no longer need to talk about being gay so we can talk about other things.

'I generally walk into choir miserable and as I spend more time there I tend to get happier. Nine nights out of ten I walk out of choir feeling a lot better than I did when I walked in, even to the point that it is hard to relax when I get home as there is so much relief from the anxiety and depression. I feel good for a change. It's partly the singing but it's also being in a relaxed, comfortable environment. Sense of humour is really important for me with my mental health and coping with life and acceptance and all the difficulties, with injustice and cruelty.'

He underscores the power of singing in a group.

'I feel the music allows for this. It unites people. It's a happy space where a lot of people joke and have a good time. There's still a serious aspect—the music director tries to move the music along but at the same time, it is a creative time. It's also intimate, matching pitch and timing and lyrics, and it is a great way to engage with people that's not so in your face. It's deep and intimate and not oppositional or confrontational.

'I felt isolated before I joined the choir. The brilliant thing about my group is that I can come and sit and be with people and feel close to them without necessarily having to engage so much. It's because you are working on something together. It's a shared experience. There's less pressure to live up to social expectations, to perform, to make polite conversation or any of that. All of that stuff is not very important to the choir. All you need to do is turn up, sit down, follow along. People won't judge you, and the music director will guide you. The thing is you do pick up the music, and the more you do, the more you start to enjoy it. It's a natural happiness thing and I find my mood just increases by engaging in the music. It's therapeutic, and the relationships that develop just happen, very casually. When I first arrived I only spoke to a couple of people as I felt so insular and I didn't want to talk to people. I was a bit scared but the relationships just crept in without me realising it.

'Now, even when I have times where I am feeling anxious and depressed, I tell myself that I don't have to perform and engage with people—all I need to do is sit down and participate. Even if I don't feel like singing, I can listen and it goes into my subconscious. To take the pressure off my anxiety, I often say to myself, "It's okay, I only need to do the possible" and I come along with that attitude all the time, and tend to enjoy it.'

He wants to promote to newcomers what our choirs can do.

'I'd like to say it really doesn't take long to fit in … It doesn't take long to learn the music … It doesn't take long to know you are part of making a beautiful sound.

It's a shared experience, singing together. It's a beautiful thing.'

There's this line in a song my choir performs, 'May you always be our shelter, may we always live in peace.' It's an Eric Bogle lyric that lingers.

∩ORTHCOTE BOY

Interview with
G R A E M E   D O Y L E
by
P H I L I P   H E U Z E N R O E D E R

as part of the Wild@heART community arts
documentary project on mental illness culture

It's been hard but what can you do?

I'm a sprung chook—I'm 67 years old and let's say I tend to over do it. My name's Graeme Doyle: artist, poet, songwriter.

My head's such a volatile thing, it's like a bushfire in there. I've had mental illness going back to when the institutions were pretty ugly inside. They've changed over the years. Now I'm in an aged care facility, which is the best asylum I've ever been in. I sort of landed on my feet. I'm friends with other residents and I like it and I'm happy. I do my work—drawings of mazes, labyrinths and intricate blocks of colour. I work hard, as hard as I can and if I stop it's only to renew myself. But you need experiences too—you can't just lock yourself in your room, because you've got no stimulation. I go into the park looking for birds or dogs, and I study the faces of fellow patients here.

I'm a Northcote boy. My father built a factory in our backyard, so my first work was helping in there. When I was 18 I went to Swinburne Technical College to do a certificate of art. And during that year I had my first breakdown in the classroom. It was a costume class, and I just snapped inside. Something broke somewhere and I went into shock and I walked home in that condition. Five miles. I went in the back door and my father was there, and I said, 'I've thrown a fit Dad'. In response he just packed up the chess game he was playing, and went into the next room. He couldn't face it. Mum realised that something was terribly wrong, and she took me to a GP. They put me into Larundel. As soon as they administered the drugs, my sanity returned, and the shock stopped. So I was very grateful for that, because I had felt like I was being tortured. It's a bushfire inside my head.

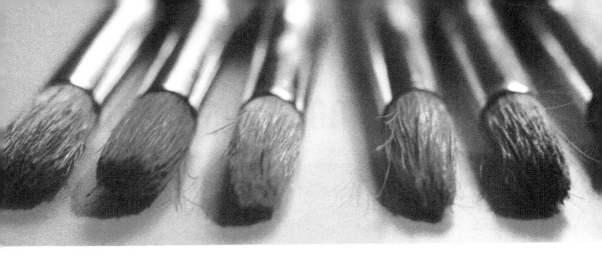

You've gotta live, you've gotta just keep going. I'm as tough as nails really, or as tough as snails, tough as tails, I'm not sure. I bounce back; I'm resilient.

I went back and got a degree and a postgraduate diploma in art. I've always kept my art going over the years. It's very, very important to me. It's a profound obsession, and people who know me would say I just didn't function without it. If I couldn't work, I'd wait until I could work and then work again. I can't put in that intensity all the time though. You just can't—your body breaks down and your mind breaks down, but I go back to it as soon as I can.

I've always tried to exhibit work too, and have even had it exhibited in the Australian National Gallery in Canberra, in an exhibition called 'A New Generation'. That may have been the peak of my career.

It's important, especially with the mental illnesses I've had, to keep your brain ticking over. I could easily become a vegetable if I didn't push myself. I have both physical and mental illnesses, including schizo-affective disorder, diabetes, chronic renal failure, diseased liver, high blood pressure, high cholesterol and a damaged thyroid.
But apart from that—no dramas! I'm fit as a fiddle!

I used to read Nietzsche years ago, about how hard he used to work despite how ill he was with a rather horrendous possible mental illness. He possibly had syphilis too. A great philosopher though, I suppose. My art, my writing, my song writing, like Nietzsche's work, it's what I'm about. It's my identity ticket so to speak.

TASH'S ACKNOWLEDGEMENTS

This book would not have been possible without the love and support of my parents, particularly my mother Marion Bernard who supported her own mother through the ups and downs of schizophrenia.

Oma, this book is for you. If only you knew how many stories you have inspired to be shared.

Thank you to Jessica Wilkinson, Lecturer in Creative and Professional Writing at RMIT, who was an invaluable resource for linking us up with keen and enthusiastic creative writing students—Natasha Rubinstein, Ella Mittas, Conor Hutchinson, Zoe Blain and Kiah Meadows. Your work is so much appreciated and shows it takes a village to raise a book! A big shout out especially to the creative and enthusiastic Kathrine Clarke—from the first moment we meet you in that tiny café in Melbourne, you have been dedicated to highlighting mental health from an Indigenous Australian perspective.

These stories are dedicated to all the hard working mental health staff and organisations who seek to highlight mental status in our community. Thank you to contacts from the Black Dog Institute, Children of Parents of Mental Illness, Wild@heART Community Arts, Men's Shed, The Butterfly Foundation, Anxiety Recovery Centre Victoria, Beyond Blue, SANE Australia, Head Space, Peter James Centre, Think Act Change, Aussie Helpers, PANDA, the Brisbane Lesbian and Gay Pride Choir and 3mate7seas.

It's an incredible thing to share deeply personal stories and we appreciate the honesty of all of our contributors. Bess Meredith, your account of depression touched us deeply and we hope it helps many other young sufferers. Doug Cox, we hope your story helps to share your experience with your family. To Bonnie Ryan, this book became more than just a book when my mother met up with you and found common ground and comfort in knowing that she was not alone. To Benjamin Robinson for reminding me 'Never doubt that a small group of thoughtful, committed, citizens can change the world. Indeed, it is the only thing that ever has.' ... We hope this book does just that. To the story contributors and interviewees, thank you for sharing so much of yourselves that will connect with so many others.

Thanks to Nicholas Walton-Healey for taking the time to go out and take honest and beautiful portraits of Bonnie and Serena, Andrea Hayes from Outbackscapes Gallery for providing your stunning landscapes that capture country Australia, to Martin Murray and Bessie Blore for proving vital contacts in our rural communities. Without your knowledge and help there would not have been a strong rural voice in the book.

Last but not least I want to say thank you with all my heart to my loving husband Michael. Though you are not a volunteer on this book, I feel you have lived and listened to every story with me. Thank you for your support and encouragement—I could not have done this without you.

To all the families, carers, friends and mental health staff—you are not alone. I hope these stories will allow you to feel connected to a larger community. Thank you for your honesty and courage in sharing your stories in the hope that we can decrease the stigma of mental illness.

PUBLISHER'S ACKNOWLEDGEMENTS

Enormous amounts of gratitude to the patient, creative and classy Leigh Rubin for your stunning design. We love you! Thanks also to your partner, Luke Gamon, for letting us occupy your time and energy for so long (and for letting you blow up his face to a double-page spread!)

Thanks to Emily Stewart, Nicola Muller, Paige Farrell and Kate O'Donnell for your developmental editing. And especially to Sarah Coull—thank you for taking on this challenge and coming through for us so beautifully and with such grace.

And last but not least our enormous thanks to the team of volunteers—proofreaders Jasmeet Sahi, Alison Strumberger, Elizabeth Whiley, Josh Arandt, Loran McDougall and Nicola, brilliant Rag & Bone board members Susanna Julian and Julian de Hoog, Kirsten Dickinson for hours of dictating long interviews, Josh our trusty and reliable writer and editorial assistant, Dan Christie for your bleach-based childhood and creative advice, and Katie Elliot for your passionate PR work, as always!

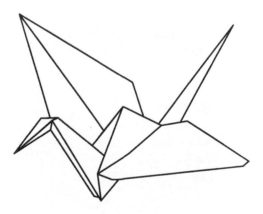

IMAGE CREDITS

We'd like to acknowledge Leigh Rubin, Luke Gamon, Andrea Hayes, David Rennie, Nicholas Walton-Healey, Caitlin Mills, Kathrine Clarke, Bess Meredith, Mic Eales, Anne Riggs and Tjeerd Tijhof for their amazing photographs that are used in the book. And our sincere thanks to our contributors who provided photos from their personal family archives.

Also, the following, thanks to Flickr and Creative Commons:
'Driftwood fire 2' by Mike Fernwood
'smoking' by Francois Karm
'Tulips from Amsterdam' by David Sim
'Liverpool Street station corwd blur' by David Sim
'Reflection' by Fe Ilya
'cold' by Acy Varlan
'Swell' by Fe Ilya
'Man on the edge' by Matt Preston
'Pelican Waters bushfire' by thinboyfatter
'Williamstown Storm NYE09' by Rob Deutscher
'Jogger in blue shorts' by Nadine Spizzirri
'One big circle, day 04' by Steven Worster
'23/366: You know what I mean' by Karrie Nodalo
'Bananas' by Steve Hopson
'Potatoes-Kipfler' by Glenn
':-D' by Emily
'Vernal equinox loaves' by Bart Everson
'The agony of choice' by Dan Taylor
'Sousveillance' by Chris Gladis
'4 miles' by bronx
'Escape from the light' by Stig Nygaard
'Fireworks' by SG
'2008.11.12 – the letter' by Adrian Clark
'Waves' by Gonzalo Diaz Fornaro
'Paintbrushes' by John Morgan